The Thought of Death
and the
Memory of War

D1611963

THE THOUGHT OF DEATH
and the
MEMORY OF WAR

Marc Crépon

Translated by Michael Loriaux
Foreword by Rodolphe Gasché

UNIVERSITY OF MINNESOTA PRESS

MINNEAPOLIS • LONDON

This work, published as part of a program providing publication assistance, received financial support from the French Ministry of Foreign Affairs, the Cultural Services of the French Embassy in the United States, and FACE (French American Cultural Exchange). See www.frenchbooknews.com.

French Voices logo designed by Serge Bloch

Originally published in French as *Vivre avec: La pensée de la mort et la mémoire des guerres*. Copyright 2008 by Éditions Hermann.

English translation copyright 2013 by the Regents of the University of Minnesota

Published by the University of Minnesota Press
111 Third Avenue South, Suite 290
Minneapolis, MN 55401-2520
http://www.upress.umn.edu

Library of Congress Cataloging-in-Publication Data

Crépon, M. (Marc).
[Vivre avec. English]
The thought of death and the memory of war / Marc Crépon ; translated by Michael Loriaux ; foreword by Rodolphe Gasché.
ISBN 978-0-8166-8005-4 (hc) — ISBN 978-0-8166-8006-1 (pb)
1. Death. 2. War. I. Title.
BD444.C7313 2013
128'.5—dc23
2013014538

Printed in the United States of America on acid-free paper

The University of Minnesota is an equal-opportunity educator and employer.

20 19 18 17 16 15 14 13   10 9 8 7 6 5 4 3 2 1

Contents

Foreword

Rodolphe Gasché

Since Socrates shared his thoughts about death with his friends before his execution in the *Phaedo,* death and sharing thoughts thereon have been a continuous concern in Western thought. Despite its seeming innovations, the thesis about death that Martin Heidegger advanced in 1927 in his opus magnum *Being and Time* is in many regards still part and parcel of the tradition inaugurated by Greek philosophy. According to this tradition, death is something that the philosopher welcomes—as Hannah Arendt says, the philosopher is somehow in love with death—since death is, precisely, what allows the soul to separate from the body, and to finally become what it most properly is, free from all the interferences and demands of the senses. By making Being-toward-death the ultimate existential structure of *Dasein,* the only one that allows for *Dasein*'s authenticity, Heidegger, all differences considered, continues the Platonic motif of "the care of the soul," according to which philosophy consists of preparing for death, which is also always the philosopher's own death. Paradoxically, Heidegger's elaborations on death occur in a work that displays only a few explicit traces, or memories, of the thoroughly unsettling and traumatic event of World War I. That same event, however, provoked a radical questioning by numerous European intellectuals of certitudes and values that until then had been considered unshakable. Heidegger's work thus became the confrontational reference point for a large part of twentieth-century philosophical thought, before and after World War II, that explicitly seeks to come to grips with the horrors of the wars and their innumerable deaths. That confrontation is due not least of all to the Platonic underpinnings of Heidegger's thought on death. His thesis about death encountered repeated resistance. Many of the major French philosophers of the twentieth century, from Jean-Paul Sartre to Emmanuel Levinas, vehemently refuse to share it because the massacres of World War I, first of all, but especially, the atrocities of World War II, such as the deportation and extermination of millions of human beings in the death camps, seemed to put into question all the basic presuppositions on which the philosophical understanding of death, and the sharing of its thought, rested hitherto. Undoubtedly, many of the critics who took on Heidegger's thought on death continued to subscribe to traditional philosophical norms and moves and did not always take into account the philosopher's attempt to confront the unthought of this thought with a reflection on the question of Being and, thus, to extricate philosophy from metaphysics. But, significantly enough, this criticism of Heidegger's elaboration on death in the wake of the horrors of World War II also gave rise to what I would like to characterize, using the Stranger's qualification of the discourse on being and non-being in Plato's *Sophist,* as a *gigantomachia*, a battle between gods and giants about being. Indeed, the debate set off by Heidegger's thought on death confronted the thinker of Being, who in his fundamental ontology sought to overcome Platonism, with different conceptions of death, the other, community, and so forth, by at least one later thinker who attempted another, more radical exit from what Heidegger qualified as metaphysical thought.

The French title of Marc Crépon's book, *Vivre avec,* interrogates "living with" oneself and others as mortal, as well as with the images of violent deaths of faceless human beings with which today's media regularly bombard us. *The Thought of Death and the Memory of War* is not only a profound meditation on what constitutes evil and a rigorous and illuminating reflection on death, community, and world; it is above all a history of a decisive segment in contemporary thought that is determined by this debate with Heidegger's thought on death. What happened in France, once Heidegger's writings became known, differs considerably from the discussions that *Being and Time* provoked in Germany after its publication, which did not so much concern the question of death as Heidegger's conception of being-with. Karl Löwith is a case in point. If Marc Crépon provides us with a new interpretation of the history of continental philosophical thought, it is because the continuous critical debate that arose after the war in France about *Being and Time* is above all one on Heidegger's thought on death. Now, what immediately strikes one about this history of the debate between the French thinkers and the German philosopher's understanding of Being-toward-death are the high standards that preside over it. None of its participants ever exploits, as is commonly the case today not only in the media but in academia as well, the scandal around Heidegger's collaboration in the thirties with the national-socialist regime in order to skirt the philosophical seriousness of his thesis. Indeed, if all these thinkers entered into a sustained argument with Heidegger's conception of *Dasein*'s relation to its death, it is not because of Heidegger's undeniable sympathies with the regime, of which, by the way, all French thinkers were already aware even during the war years, but because the violence of the two wars and the systematic annihilation of millions of people put philosophical thought as such, particularly insofar as it concerns death and the sharing of that thought, radically into question. Already for Freud, the disillusion caused by World War I affected all the claims made by humanity in the name of culture. If numerous thinkers in the wake of what happened during, and continues to happen ever since, World War II systematically took on Heidegger's thought on death with exemplary seriousness and rigor—that is, with the impeccable fairness that *as a thinker* Heidegger deserves—it is because the realities of the massacres have put into question a certain traditional conception of philosophical thought. The urgency of a response to Heidegger's notion of Being-toward-death, whose stakes, tellingly, bear on the possibility of living together at all—that is, living in a world that is based on a politics grounded in ethics—is such that it allows for no spectacular, and more often than not cheap, condemnation of its author. Indeed, the self-righteous dismissal of a philosophical thesis because of its thinker's collaboration serves in the end only to avoid facing what the horrors of the past century have done to our conception of philosophical thought, and to reaffirm conventional modes of thinking and values that the events have thoroughly shaken in their very foundations. Further, the urgency to rethink thought from the ground up is all the more pressing since, in fact, Heidegger's thesis on death was an intrinsic aspect of his own attempt at overcoming philosophical thought toward a more fundamental, and non-metaphysical, way of thinking, which, in light of what has been experienced and witnessed during the twentieth century, has been judged not to have gone far enough.

At stake in Heidegger's conception of the Being-toward-death as a fundamental existential structure of *Dasein* is the experience of death as the annihilation of Being. Undoubtedly, since in Being-toward-death *Dasein* relates to the annihilation that always already holds sway within Being itself, Being-toward-death opens *Dasein* also to Being itself. What death means in this context would thus require careful and nuanced consideration. Yet the death toward which *Dasein* is exposed is also that of the individual *Dasein*'s annihilation understood in the sense of a sheer ceasing to *be*. Let us recall that for Heidegger *Dasein* is from the start a being-with-others. At all moments and times *Dasein*'s existence is determined by its relations to others. Such being-with-others is one in which *Dasein,* in the average way of its Being, shares everything with them. Since death sets it apart from all others in that my own death cannot be experienced by others in my place, only the possibility of death represents the condition, if explicitly assumed and acknowledged as that which alone is truly mine, that allows for *Dasein*'s individualization or, rather, singularization and, hence, for its authentic being. This possibility of Being-toward-death as the only possibility that is properly my own, which inexorably derives from the very way Heidegger conceives of being-with-others, dissolves all relations to others and sets *Dasein* radically apart from all community with the "they." It follows from this understanding of death in *Being and Time* that the death of the other cannot in truth be experienced, that one can relate to it only from the outside and talk about it only by way of clichés. As a result, no community founded on the other's mortality is conceivable.

Opening with an analysis of Freud's meditations in the wake of World War I on the disillusions created by the barbarisms of war and the sobering experience that death is not something that happens only to anonymous others but can also happen to me, *The Thought of Death and the Memory of War* intimates, however implicitly, that the philosophical thesis concerning Being-toward-death as *Dasein*'s most proper possibility, notwithstanding the near lack of references to the war, is Heidegger's response to what the war had made it inevitable to acknowledge: no denial by the civilized masses can in the end do away with mortality. Yet, another even bloodier and more violent war was necessary to trigger the systematic critique of Heidegger's thought on *Dasein*'s mortality. Because such a critique was made difficult by the intellectual and moral climate in the period between the two wars in which most German intellectuals, whatever their orientation, shared many of the presuppositions underlying Heidegger's analysis, the debate whose history Crépon reconstructs in a most rigorous and admirable way in his book, which is essentially French, became only truly possible during and in the wake of the last war—that is, only after a broader reception of Heidegger's work in France had taken place. And, again, I think it is necessary to repeat that, even then, the critique by many thinkers of Heidegger's thought on death was not motivated by any "Heidegger scandal" but, rather, by the difficult philosophical legacy of *Being and Time*—that is, the legacy of the philosophical presuppositions and implications of the thought on death for conceiving of community, ethics, and politics.

One of the significant achievements of *The Thought of Death and the Memory of War* is to have reminded us of the seminal role in the debate played by Jean-Paul Sartre, who in 1943—that is, still during the occupation of France—proposed in *Being and Nothingness* a detailed, critical discussion of the relevant chapters from *Being and Time* devoted to Being-toward-death. If I linger for a brief moment on the main objections in Sartre's work (including all his plays) to Heidegger's contention that the possibility of death is what is properly mine, it is not only because of their continued resonance in the writings of later thinkers on Heidegger's understanding of death, such as Paul Ricœur and Emmanuel Levinas, but also because these objections put into place a positive framework in which a political dimension is restituted to death by the fact that others will judge about the meaning of my death and that I myself will decide about the meaning of the death of others, as well. Sartre's prime objection to Heidegger is that death cannot be appropriated and that it cannot ever become something that I could claim as mine. Indeed, by arguing that death is what disappropriates me of myself, that is, of the entirety of the possibilities that are mine, he opposes Heidegger by disclosing the utterly absurd nature of death. But, paradoxically, it is precisely this lack of meaning that death has for me that, according to Sartre, opens the possibility of *dying for* a cause in the hope of reversing death's absurdity and of linking death again in an essential way to the existence of others whose opinions are instrumental in establishing the meaningfulness, or lack thereof, of my death. Needless to say, since in the end it is always the other who triumphs in judging whether I have died a qualified death by dying for a cause, death remains irreducibly absurd. Yet this dependence on others who will judge whether I died meaningfully implies also that during my lifetime I entertain a relation to the death of others that is even more essential than the one to my own death. If the meaning of death is a function of others, it follows that while I am alive I am responsible for the memory of others and, thus, for the meaningfulness, or lack thereof, of their death. As Crépon notes, to live is always to *live with*—that is, to share life with others and, beyond their life, with the dead others in the memory of their life and death. In short, Sartre's critique of the mineness of death not only reconnects it to the others with whom one shares life but also highlights a responsibility that I have with respect to the other's death.

This is certainly not the place to discuss in detail all the thinkers who, as Crépon demonstrates, have taken issue with Heidegger's thought on death. Broadly speaking, all of them make a strong case for the experience of the death of the other and the responsibility I incur with respect to the dead and their memory, which Heidegger relegated to the margins in his inquiry into *Dasein*'s own death. At the beginning of this foreword, I referred to the *gigantomachia* that Heidegger's thought on death did not fail to provoke. Indeed, inasmuch as Levinas submitted Heidegger's propositions about death as constitutive of *Dasein*'s authenticity, wholeness, and self-sameness to an interminable debate throughout his work, propositions made inacceptable by the memory of the Second World War, and in particular the Shoah, is it not Levinas who, in this case, figures as the Platonic Stranger that, in the *Sophist,* proceeded to an all-out parricidal confrontation with Parmenides in an attempt to overhaul the Platonic thought of identity? Levinas's challenge to Heidegger's conception of death is certainly highly complex and multilayered in that he puts a different aspect of this conception into question in each of the

numerous texts that he has devoted to the issue. Rather than his prob-
lematization of the conception of death as my first and foremost possibility, the privilege of anxiety in relation to my death, the heroism
that is involved in authenticity, the solipsist closure of the self on
itself in its relation to its death, and so forth, I will only highlight here
his criticism of Heidegger's understanding of death as annihilation—
that is, as the termination of being. Levinas's criticism of all the aspects
of death set forth in *Being and Time*, including the one to which he
devotes most of his criticism—*Dasein*'s singularization in the face of
its death and the subsequent breaking of all ties with others—is, indeed, framed by his contestation of the primacy of ontology in Heidegger's thought on death. By defining death as the impossibility of
all possibilities, as annihilation, that is, as the return to nothingness,
death is understood as the privation of Being. Differently put, by thinking of death in relation to the question of Being, death is identified,
fixed in its meaning, and everything that is radically other, unknowable, and scandalous about it is evacuated from it. Undoubtedly, in
his debate with Heidegger's existential analytic and *Dasein*'s relation
to death, Levinas seeks to display and uproot the analytic in question
by doing justice to all the aspects of death that it did not deem necessary to take into consideration, such as the relation of suffering and
death, the possibility of me dying at the hands of an other (of murder, in short), or my decision to die for the sake, or in the place, of
someone else—that is, in sacrifice. As Crépon argues, this criticism
targets not only the very principle of ontology that subtends Heidegger's existential analytic of death but also the primacy of ontology in
Western thought in general, including Heidegger's fundamental ontology. Indeed, to Heidegger's claim that death toward which *Dasein* exists is most properly its own, Levinas opposes an experience of death's
radical alterity. Since, for Levinas, it is something the subject can in
no way appropriate and on which the subject has no leverage what-
soever, death can, therefore, never be identified and determined in

its essence. Since death remains an unknown that cannot be linked meaningfully to the whole of one's life, let alone make it whole, it is impervious to the alternative of Being and Nothingness. To argue that death is *Dasein*'s ownmost possibility and the condition of its authenticity and being properly itself amounts essentially to a denial of death's alterity.

Although not explicitly acknowledged by Levinas himself, by beginning with the suffering that another human being's death causes in the subject in order to start accounting for the experience of death, the ground is laid, as Crépon points out, for an analysis of the responsibility that everyone incurs in the face of the death of another—an analysis for which there is no room if death is most properly my own. The agonizing other unmistakably calls for help and asks to be taken care of, thus obliging me to stand by him or her. When the other demands from me protection and help in delaying death, a structure that Crépon calls "being-against-death" comes into view that intimately links the experience of death to relations and circumstances that are in essence social. Further, the other's face also resists experiencing death as annihilation—that is, as a passage from being into nothingness. More precisely, the face of the other is the index of the moral impossibility of annihilation in the first place. Undoubtedly, all the crimes against humanity during World War II have proved that there has been a systematic will to annihilate and to condemn others to inexistence. By highlighting murder in his meditations on death, however, Levinas also suggests that the deliberate will to wipe out millions and millions of human beings, including the memory of their existence, cannot morally be achieved, thus putting Heidegger's understanding of death as framed by the alternative between being and nothingness even more radically into question. By starting to reflect on death as originating in murder, death is unswervingly inscribed within the sphere of being-with-others rather than being linked to the problematic of ontology. If the other's murderous will is the source of my death, my death will never have been my own. Yet, while the other is the hostile other from whom death may strike me and who prevents me from being alone responsible for my death, the face of the other as I experience it, Levinas contends, is also what prohibits murder and makes the possibility of annihilation *de jure* impossible. The responsibility that I have before and for the other entirely displaces the relation that I have to my own death and the threat that it poses to me. The face of the other makes me responsible for living up to the interdiction of murder that it expresses. His or her vulnerability has priority over the concern with my own death.

Levinas's analyses of the relation to the other, as a result of which all identity and self-sameness of the self are rendered entirely dependent on the other, serve to replace ontology with ethics as first philosophy. This is what motivates me to characterize Levinas's battle with Heidegger and the whole of Western thought from Plato on as a *gigantomachia* in which Heidegger's attempt to overcome metaphysics by way of a fundamental ontology and the question of Being is, in turn, overcome by a more radical dismantling of the principle of ontology through ethical philosophy. By tying the reflection on death to the threat that comes from the other and the simultaneous interdiction of murder by the face of the other, the problematic of death not only shifts from me toward the other, thus linking it in an essential manner to the interpersonal fabric of being-with-others, but on a deeper level such a reflection also displaces all ontological concern with sameness, identity, and selfhood in the direction of the question of alterity, and the difference that the other makes.

In Crépon's engaging outline of the debate produced by Heidegger's thought of death primarily in French but also in Czech philosophy, Derrida's critical discussion of both Heidegger's and Levinas's respective positions figures as a special moment. The presentation of Derrida's debate with both thinkers is preceded by provocative chapters that inquire into thought's responsibility in relation to the memory of the victims of the wars of the twentieth century, into how, according to Jan Patočka, the meaning of the world is intrinsically a function of the relation to the dead, and, finally, into Ricœur's conception of "accompanying" of the other at the moment of approaching death, thus mobilizing all the resources of life in a continuing affirmation of it—all of which succeed in bringing the eminently ethical and political dimension of the question of death into greater and greater relief. By positioning the dense chapters devoted to Derrida toward the end of the book, Crépon not only situates a decisive aspect of the latter's thought within the history sketched out and shows it to have been the latest development of the question that has driven this history, but the order of the book also obeys additional reasons that need to be briefly addressed here.

According to our most common understanding, ethics regulates, first and foremost, our relations to the entirety of living others, whereas our relations to the dead in mourning, and the ways we share mourning with others, are understood to make up only a restricted domain within the totality of the relations to which ethics applies. Yet Derrida takes issue from the start with what within ethics separates and disjoins the relation to the living and the memory of the dead on the grounds that such a separation presupposes a self-identical self that is affected by its relations to others in merely an exterior fashion. By putting this assumption radically in question, by showing that the self is always already constituted by the trace of the other within itself, Derrida, Crépon argues, deconstructs what within traditional ethics separates the living from the dead. Indeed, since the other is by definition a mortal and finite other, the trace of the other that constitutes all self implies that the self is always already, from the beginning, that is, in an originary way, in mourning—in a mourning that does not have to wait for an other (close or not) to disappear. It follows that an ethics based on hospitality, such as the one of Levinas, is intimately interconnected with an ethics that starts with the self if such a self is in its very essence—that is, structurally—indebted to an other whom it always already mourns. As Crépon observes, with this insight into an originary mourning we touch on the acme of Derrida's confrontation with the thought of Levinas, namely, the demonstration that the principle of ethics is double, structuring both the relation of self to itself and to others in indissociable fashion. As Crépon's elucidation of the impressive complexity of Derrida's argument against Levinas's thought on death shows, Derrida does not at all put into question the subject's responsibility toward the death of the other that Levinas opposes to Heidegger's thesis of the mineness of death; yet, by recognizing an originary mourning at the heart of the self and its relation to its own death, Derrida questions the rigor of the partition that neatly distinguishes between the relation to one's own death and to that of the other. Hospitality and mourning the death of both the other and oneself are intrinsically linked. Further, if this is the case, then the opposition between the thought on death by Heidegger and Levinas, and ultimately between ontology and ethics, can no longer simply be taken for granted either.

As one knows from the relevant chapters in *Being and Time* on *Dasein*'s relation to death, Heidegger does not consider mourning to be one of the existential structures of Being-in-the-world. Yet, when discussing these chapters in *Aporias,* Derrida intimates that the theme of mourning (lacking in Heidegger's considerations) may have a political dimension. Crépon devotes the last chapters of *The Thought of Death and the Memory of War* to eloquently teasing out this political dimension, arguing that the sharing of a responsibility to the dead is in the very service of life as, indeed, a powerful affirmation of life as mortal life. But to conclude this foreword let me ask whether Derrida's development with respect to Levinas's primacy of the other, and hence of ethics in philosophy, does not bear in the same way on Heidegger's stress on *Dasein* in isolation from others and, hence, on the ontological framework in which his account of Being-toward-death is situated.

Let us bear in mind that *Dasein* as Being-in-the-world is from the start a being that is with others, more precisely, in a community with the "they." However, *Dasein*'s Being-toward-death, that is, toward its own annihilation, if assumed as such, makes it possible for *Dasein* to be that possibility that no one other can be in its place and, thus, to be authentically itself—in short, a singular *Dasein*. Two things need to be stressed here: on the one hand, *Dasein* is with others only to the extent that it also has the possibility of a radical singularization in the face of the death that it alone will suffer; on the other hand, it is only qua being-with-others that *Dasein* can withdraw from all relations with them in its relation to its ownmost proper possibility. Yet, if this is the case, does it not also follow that *Dasein*'s specific wholeness given by its radical and authentic individuation—a wholeness that, admittedly, is not based on self-identity but, paradoxically, on a structural mode of Being that points away from itself toward its annihilation—is necessarily inhabited by the trace of the other? Undoubtedly, the other is, first, inauthentic, an other among the "they" in distinction from the self that resolutely takes its mortality upon itself. But this other is in denial of its finitude only to the extent that, precisely, it is mortal, and that in such a way its death has, in Blanchot's words (expressly referred to by Derrida in this context) always already occurred. Yet, independently of whether Heidegger makes room for mourning in his existential analytic of *Dasein,* this inevitable relation to the other as mortal and of singularized *Dasein* to itself as mortal, having already died in advance of death, as it were, also inevitably makes a certain mourning into a structural condition of *Dasein*'s singularizing relation to its own death.

In conclusion, I return to the history fostered in French philosophy by the controversy over Heidegger's propositions about death. Apart from the protracted criticism of all the aspects of Heidegger's thesis about death, Levinas's critique stands out within this debate inasmuch as it expressly takes issue with the whole ontological framework of

Western philosophy, including Heidegger's attempt to overcome this tradition by way of a fundamental reflection on the question of Being. The debate between Heidegger and Levinas has all the characteristics of a *gigantomachia*—that is, of a war about the question of whether first philosophy is ontology or ethics. But how, then, to characterize Derrida's debate with both Heidegger's and Levinas's reflections on death, on self and other, on mourning and hospitality, on ontology and ethics? What is the effect on the history in question of a reflection that not only exposes the shortcomings of Heidegger's account of death as a singularizing possibility of *Dasein*, but also, at the same time, confronts Levinas's thought on death as primarily the death of the other with the insight that the self's relation to itself is also already mourning its own death? If *The Thought of Death and the Memory of War* shows Derrida to be, for the moment at least, the last one to have taken up the debate that Heidegger's thought on death has provoked, and if he has done so in taking issue with both Heidegger's characterization of death and Levinas's critique of it, does this not entail that Derrida, in a way, has brought the debate and its history to an end, to its completion? Does this not also imply that with Derrida the strict distinction and tension between ontology and ethics have become problematic and, thus, also that all *gigantomachia* as a staged scenery for the intraphilosophical debate from Plato to the present concerning the very principles of philosophy has, at least for the moment, become groundless?

However, to suggest that the extremely fruitful and decisive debate may have ended with Derrida's reflections on both Heidegger's and Levinas's thought on death does not mean that the stakes of this debate have been laid to rest. As Crépon repeatedly reminds us throughout the book, death makes up the news—the death of countless faceless or anonymous others whose images have the effect of eclipsing the singularity of the victims' death and, thus, also the end of the world as such that each death signifies. *The Thought of Death and the*

Memory of War is a call to resist such images in which death is no longer death since it happens mainly to anonymous others, and to confront death instead as something that is utterly singular for each of the victims involved. But to experience death as thoroughly singular presupposes being-with-others in a community capable of a "we" that is not exclusive but open to all—in short, being-with-others in an endless struggle for a world in which sharing death would amount to an affirmation of life. It is toward such a community, such a "we," and such a world that *The Thought of Death and the Memory of War* is on the way.

War and the Death Drive

≫ SIGMUND FREUD ≪

However we judge the past or the future, our judgment will be haunted, marked by the seal of war in the twentieth century. The memory of war intervenes inescapably in the relations among states, whether bringing them together or driving them apart. It gives rise, year after year, at predetermined dates and in predetermined places, to appeals for forgiveness, symbolic gestures of reconciliation, just as, here and there, it is used to recall unpaid debts and persistent misapprehensions, as well as absolutions that wait enduringly upon unuttered pleas for forgiveness. Our memory on occasion abides in some or other survival of prejudice, in the characterizations and caricatures of "peoples" that are propagated in wartime. The memory of war, in the form of commemorations, punctuates our political calendar with its most "sacred" dates—November 11, June 6 and 18, and May 8 in France. On such dates the memory of war is essentially the memory of those who died in war, the recollection of lives sacrificed, etched in the stone of "war memorials" and in the bronze of commemorative plaques— which governments, in the wake of conflicts, have always erected as reminders, as factors, or *instruments* of cohesion, and sometimes of "union sacrée" and mobilization. Finally, the memory of war is inflicted on us, over and over again, as an element of political discourse and action. Memory, by this very fact, informs the judgments we make of one another. Because memory can be insulted, wounded,

outraged; because it lends itself to falsification, to denials and dene-
gations; because it is rendered fragile as much by the possibility of
being forgotten as by that of being instrumentalized, memory becomes the object of ethical as well as political responsibility. The his-
torian cannot adequately address this responsibility. One can neither
do just *anything with* nor do *nothing with* memory; one can neither
make just *anything from* nor *nothing from* memory. So why do we
remember wars? Why does *their* remembrance occupy so much space
in the collective imaginary? Why are we dealing with something very
different from historical knowledge, however necessary this might
be? Because memory as responsibility is about our *past, present, and
future attitude toward death*.

    Freud would suggest as much in a 1915 text, *Zeitgemässes über Krieg
und Tod*, or *Reflections on War and Death*, written when World War I
had been raging for more than a year already, though (nearly all) the
worst was still to come.[1] Future decades would not controvert his
reflections. As he endeavored to analyze why the evil was experienced "with excessive force" in war—and we know that, with the
passage of time, that excess would not abate—Freud pointed to the
convergence of two phenomena: the disillusionment that war induced,
and the change in our attitude toward death that war engendered.
The one and the other shall serve as my point of departure.

What caused disillusionment? Like many who followed him, Freud
explains that disillusionment was provoked by the incapacity of the
belligerents' *common civilization*—that great humanistic civilization
that had given to the nations of Europe their titles of nobility—to
efface or contain the transformation of the foreigner into the enemy.
That incapacity was aggravated by the inability to slow the pace at
which, from that point forward, *another civilization*—one characterized by hostility, hatred, and repulsion—asserted itself and prevailed

against the moral and political "restrictions" that were the legacy of humanism:

> It [war] places itself above all the restrictions pledged in times of peace, the so-called rights of nations, it does not acknowledge the prerogatives of the wounded and of the physicians, the distinction between peaceful and fighting members of the population, or the claims of private property. It hurls down in blind rage whatever bars its way, as though there were to be no future and no peace after it is over. It tears asunder all community bonds among the struggling peoples and threatens to leave a bitterness which will make impossible any re-establishment of these ties for a long time to come.[2]

Exposed to the disastrous impact of filtered news [*information*] and monitored communications (instruments of this *other civilization*), encouraged to approve if not to acclaim the violation of moral principles whose transgression they could not have imagined they would one day accept, nothing in their history, their traditions, art, literature, law, or medicine stopped those whom Freud calls "the participants in humanity's highest civilization" from surrendering to "cruelty"— however one might define it. Cruelty, as we shall see below, is not unrelated to the complex question of "change in the relation to death."

The author of *The Interpretation of Dreams* was assuredly not the only one to witness disillusionment on such an unprecedented scale. As we know, the echo of that disillusionment reverberated more forcefully as the century progressed and as the mass of victims swelled to millions upon millions. Our present time, still today, is fashioned from these reverberations, however diverse the traces (artistic, literary, historical, and even statistical) that evince their resonance. The echo was perceptible, as early as the 1930s, in the shadow cast by, among other things, the persecutions whose victims were the Jewish communities, first, of Germany, then, of the greater part of Europe.

So many witnesses, so many images of suffering and destruction congregate around this persecution that they make *an illusion* of any civilization—that is, of any moral and political system—that will not invoke them or answer for them.

Freud's *Reflections on War and Death* already speaks of "disillusionment." But disillusionment can occur only against the backdrop of some prior illusion. What is the nature of this "first" [*première*] illusion? Is it the same as that evoked above? Because the following pages will measure its importance over and over again (though by following a very different path), it is appropriate to pursue our reading of Freud further and to attend to the interpretation that he provides. That interpretation emphasizes the importance of those impulses that the requirement of human community classifies as either egotistic and cruel, on the one hand, or altruistic and social on the other hand. But it does not posit the eradication of the former in favor of the latter, but rather their recomposition or transformation based on erotic additions, following a bimodal path. On the one hand, this transformation reflects a generic disposition, which all humans inherit at birth, and as such is innate. On the other hand, it is the object of an acquisition—that is, an education, imparted during the lifetime of each of us: "If we call a person's individual capacity for transforming his egotistical impulses under the influence of love his cultural adaptability, we can say that this consists of two parts, one congenital and the other acquired, and we may add that the relation of these two to each other and to the untransformed part of the emotional life is a very variable one."[3]

Under these conditions, the illusion is easily deciphered. It derives, on the one hand, from the overestimation of civilization's aptitudes, in contrast to the abidingly primitive life of impulses. It derives, on the other hand, from the conviction that our "submission to civilization" is synonymous with a definitive and irreversible "ennoblement" of the impulses—that is, that it acts in us like *a kind of second nature* that insulates us from cruelty and evil. But the variability of the innate and the acquired attest, on the contrary, to the foundational complexity, variety, and fragility of the causes [or patterns: *motifs*] of both civilizational adaptability and submission. The exaggerated confidence that we grant to both the one and the other overlooks the "ongoing impulse repression" from which, in the majority of cases, they proceed, and the reactive and compensatory manifestations that impulse repression always tends to engender, and which make our confidence illusory. Wherein lies civilization? Wherein lies the repression of cruelty and of evil? In very little. And yet we always assume that repression is more solid, more anchored in nature, than it actually is. For nothing disappears, nothing is abolished. As developed as "civilized society" might be, the egotistical and cruel tendencies (what Freud calls primitive animism) do not *go away*. Nothing prevents "the transformation of impulses upon which our aptitude for culture rests"[4] from being "defeated, whether temporarily or durably," and thus nothing prevents evil and cruelty, once unleashed, from surmounting the protective barriers that society has erected. The horrors of war, all wars, recall us to this painful truth. It forms the most unfathomable part of the memory that we retain of war. The author of *Reflections on War and Death,* in 1915, says as much in words that sound the knell of the still-future death of our illusions: "These discussions have already afforded us the consolation that our mortification and painful disappointment on account of the uncivilized behavior of our fellow world citizens in this war were not justified. They rested upon an illusion to which we had succumbed. In reality they have not sunk as deeply as we feared because they never really rose as high as we had believed."[5]

The second phenomenon that Freud relates to our feeling of strangeness in a world engulfed by the abomination of war is the way in which evil (which war—and its memory—exemplifies and propagates)

perturbs our relation to death. In the course of our lives we obviously have a tendency to shunt death off to the side, as if we cannot believe, in our own case as in that of others, in our ineluctable demise (however much sickness or bereavement of a loved one might intervene to remind us of it). War, however, brutally and cruelly amplifies the experience of death. It suspends our customary relation to death because nothing enables us to deny it any longer. Wartime is nothing other than the time of this invasion and deluge. When we preserve the memory, when we commemorate the victims, when we make of the remembrance of sacrifice an ethical and political responsibility, it is above all *this time* that is remembered: "Death is no longer to be denied; we are compelled to believe in it. People really die and no longer one by one, but in large numbers, often ten thousand in one day. It is no longer an accident. Of course, it still seems accidental whether a particular bullet strikes this man or that but the survivor may easily be struck down by a second bullet, and the accumulation of deaths ends the impression of accident."[6]

What *is recalled* from this time is not limited to this memory. If the disturbance of our attitude toward death cannot be dissociated from the disillusionment discussed above it is because both the one and the other call attention to the fiction of the "primitive man" that Freud is still calling "the man of earliest times."[7] What is the nature of primitive man's relation to death? The originality of Freud's approach consists in emphasizing two points of decisive importance. First, he places what he is trying to conceptualize as a *primitive relation to death* under the sign of a partition. On one side, primitive man had to deny the ineluctable character of his own death. He could only live by *imagining* himself to be immortal. On the other side, as soon as the question arose of putting an end to the life of another, a stranger, an enemy—that is, as soon as he derived benefit, for his own life, from annihilating that of another—this same primitive man knew very well that he had "to take death seriously" and to take full account of its consequences. Therefore, what is *primitive* in this regard is as much the evasion of death (through distractions, diversions, deflection, negation) as the possibility of murder. Second, Freud, with regard to this partition, highlights the ambivalence (and therefore the reversibility) of the place of loved ones. On the one hand—and because the attachment is irreducible—*their death* is, for the ego who loves them, a disaster from which ego struggles to recover. Each disappearance takes away part of ego's own "me"—by reminding him that "he, too, could die."[8] On the other hand, each disappearance frees him from a strangeness (that of the other) that could—nothing can rule this out—turn hostile. However much loved or cherished, the other (the loved one, the brother) was loved only for an uncertain duration (during which love could turn into hatred)—a duration that retains the trace of innumerable murders (among them the first murder of all) and which, as such, is the sign of our finitude.

Hence Freud's great lesson, without which war is inexplicable: if humanity has always *made a distinction* between those whose death brought grief, though not without ambiguity, and those whom one could see die and cause to die without being affected (as if *their* death had nothing to do with death per se; that is, *one's own* death and that of *one's own* loved ones); and if it is true that the difference, the separation, or the partition which emerged from this distinction is infinitely variable, then ethics (and politics, as we will see below) has no other object than the *becoming* or the *destiny* of this distinction:

> The first and most important prohibition of the awakening conscience declared: Thou shalt not kill. This arose as a reaction against the gratification of hate for the beloved dead which is concealed behind grief, and was gradually extended to the unloved stranger and finally also to the enemy. . . . What no human being desires to do does not have to be forbidden, it is self-exclusive. The very emphasis of the commandment: Thou shalt not kill, makes it certain that

we are descended from an endlessly long chain of generations of murderers, whose love of murder was in their blood as it is perhaps also in ours. The ethical strivings of mankind, with the strength and significance of which we need not quarrel, are an acquisition of the history of man; they have since become, though unfortunately in very variable quantities, the hereditary possessions of people of today.[9]

It is this inheritance that war puts in question, to our great bewilderment, over and over again. It effaces the culture that transmits this inheritance and escorts us back through the murderous paths of "primitive man." Freud's observation is unforgiving—and if we remember the wars of the last century, it is only because of the haunting pertinence of the four propositions that war proclaims: "*1. War strips off the deposits of civilization and allows the primitive man in us to reappear. 2. It forces us once again to be heroes who cannot believe in their own death. 3. It stamps all strangers as enemies whose death we ought to cause or wish. 4. It counsels us to rise above the death of those whom we love.*"[10]

We are far from having fully realized the ramifications of these four propositions. Freud declares, toward the end of his analysis (as if better to dispel our illusions), that we have no other solution, when confronted with the ineluctable recurrence of war (evil's tenacity), than to alter our cultural and customary attitude toward death. There is no other path available to us than the lucid and tragic recollection of this unconscious relation to death, which, he adds, "we have until now so carefully repressed."[11] We must admit to ourselves that we have become more disarmed, discouraged, if not crushed by the unleashing of the violence and cruelty that war signifies, to the extent that we have forgotten the place occupied *in this relation* by the possibility of murder. We have overestimated civilization's powers of resistance.

How do we recall to mind this possibility of murder? How would our way of life change if we took it into account? Freud, adopting an authoritarian and prophetic tone, explains that if war perdures in the world, it is because it presents itself as something shared among a plurality of peoples who are *foreign* to one another. Throughout his *Reflections on War and Death,* the figure of the *foreigner,* the *enemy,* and the question of the relation to death, are in fact inseparable. Our perception and understanding of the world's *divided* condition, on the one hand, and our attitude toward death (i.e., the death of the other—as foreigner or as enemy) on the other, cannot be examined separately. How are we to understand what binds them? Is it that, in an era that seems devoted to evil, we lack, together and conjointly, a shared *sense of the world* and a shared *sense of death*? But then, of what should this *common sense* consist? How would it be shared?

These are not questions that Freud addressed. But they emerge again and again in the work of philosophers of the last century. If it is true that the question of philosophy's inscription in its time is always an important one, the philosophy of the twentieth century is particularly inseparable from the shadow projected by war—inseparable, that is, prior to any other analytical element, from two world conflicts, the tens of millions of deaths, civilian and military, that they caused, whether on the fronts of Europe and elsewhere, or in cities, occupied or razed by bombs, or by the deportation of entire populations, or, finally and above all, by the extermination of the Jews of Europe in the death camps. If we ask what, *in* and *of* this time, unsettled philosophy, the response directs us toward what we can only call a certain "experience" of death—of death as annihilation—from which thought, whether of history, politics, ethics, justice, or even of science and technology, could not escape.

And yet it was not from the direct and explicit contemplation of the "unimaginable annihilation" of war, in all its facets, that the "thought of death" [*la pensée de la mort*], made necessary by war, emerged.[12]

The thought of death is indeed indissociable from the appearance in
1927 (the date is not insignificant) of a book, *Being and Time,* that
does not evoke war unless by allusion, nor betray, visibly at least, any
trace of World War I, which subsequent reflection on death and the
dead will be unable to ignore. This apparent indifference is not the
least of the paradoxes regarding the reception of this work. For, although the encounter with Heidegger's major work would nurture
much philosophizing in the twentieth century, before and after the
Second World War, that encounter, inhabited as it is by the memory
of war, would find in the book's analysis of Being-toward-death one
of its most challenging and decisive episodes. In *Being and Nothingness,* Sartre devotes one of his most tightly constructed analyses to
this passage.[13] Patočka's reflections on the "solidarity of the shaken,"
in *The Heretical Essays,* intertwines with the thread of Heidegger's
analyses.[14] Much of the work of Blanchot and Derrida is haunted by
these momentous paragraphs.[15] Nearer to our time, the work of Françoise Dastur pursues, through several books, a rigorous meditation
on Being-toward-death.[16] Finally, and above all, the work of Levinas,
more than that of anyone else in the second half of the last century,
inscribes its critical reading of Heidegger in the remembrance of war
and the procession of its victims.

This "critical" filiation, to which one could add the names of many
more writers and poets—beginning with that of Paul Celan—lays
out *another path* for trying to reflect on the link, placed under the sign
of a twofold responsibility (ethical and political), between the memory of war and the thought of death. Without losing sight of the questions raised by our reading of Freud (grieving, sacrifice, murder, and,
finally, the shared [*commun*] sense of the world and of death), which
will reemerge later in this volume, it is this "other" path that we shall
follow in subsequent chapters.

Being-toward-Death and
Dasein's Solitude

➤ Martin Heidegger ◄

> There is no politics of death—of death *properly speaking*. The
> existential analysis does not claim any competence (and indeed, it
> has none) for dealing with political problems of burial, of the cult of
> the dead, and, above all, of war and medicine. . . . The existential
> analysis does not want to know anything about the ghost [*revenant*]
> or about mourning.
>
> —JACQUES DERRIDA, *Aporias*

With these two phrases, as is often the case in his writings on Heidegger, Derrida opens up a perspective that is at the same time a breach.
It has been said over and over again that the existential analytic
recoils from thinking about the political, that it treats the political as
an ancillary and derivative question. But Derrida's two remarks suggest something else. They invite us to ask more specifically if this
wavering before the political might not be what is playing itself out
in the sections *Being and Time* (46–53) devoted to the existential analytic of Being-toward-death. That analysis adumbrates a question that
will emerge frequently in the thought of Sartre, Levinas, Patočka, and
others, as well as in the chapters that follow. The question concerns
our shared responsibility—indistinguishably ethical and political—
before and against death. What kind of political community is suggested or excluded by the thought of death, assuming that it is true
that such thought culminates in the idea—foreshadowed in section

74 of *Being and Time,* and which Heidegger will develop several years later in his commentary on the hymns of Hölderlin—that sacrifice constitutes the essence of that which, in its relation to death, is capable of gathering a community and founding its sharing and apportionment [*partage*]?[1]

Recall that Heidegger's first move is to dispose of two considerations. First, he shows that any historical-biographical or ethnological-psychological investigation of death that considers the existential interpretation of death[2] superfluous is insufficiently grounded. Second, he claims to demonstrate that it is impossible to turn the death [*mourir*] of the other (or the annihilation [*achèvement*] of the *Dasein* of the other) into a theme that substitutes for the analysis of *Dasein* in its totality. On this second point, one could go so far as to say that *Dasein* governs the analysis as a whole. Indeed, if Heidegger recalls at each step of his argument that *Dasein* is essentially being-with-others (*Mitsein*)—and if he reiterates this point even more frequently in the pages devoted to death—it is to emphasize more decisively that Being-toward-death marks the absolute limit of what *Dasein* can share. Death, burial, funeral rites, condolences, and the commemoration of the dead may be common experiences, but they are secondary to that which ushers *Dasein* back to its "ownmost" possibility: Being-toward-death.[3]

At the limit of what *Dasein* can share, at the limit therefore of *Mitsein,* he advances two major considerations, the first of which is the impossibility of experiencing the dying of others: "In suffering this loss, . . . we have no way of access to the loss-of-being as such which the dying man 'suffers.' The dying of others is not something we experience in a genuine sense; at most we are always just 'there alongside.'"[4]

If this experience is impossible, it is because it is impossible for me to imagine what constitutes, for the other, its "coming to the end," even though death belongs to the fundamental modes [*modalités*] of "being one-with-the-other in the same world." In fact, if one of the fundamental modes of "being one-with-the-other in the same world" is, constitutively, identifying with its preoccupation as shared preoccupation, then the relation of *Dasein* to its ownmost possibility marks the absolute limit of this identification. I can represent to myself anything of the other—and thus share anything with the other—except its own relation to its "coming to the end." Speech, gesture, fellowship, solicitude—the things whose disappearance Norbert Elias deplores in *The Loneliness of Dying*—come to a full stop before this absolute limit: the Being-toward-death of others cannot be a preoccupation that is shared. On the contrary, such sharing is absolutely inconceivable. Heidegger reminds us, laconically, "No one can take the other's dying away from him" (*keinen kann dem Anderen sein Sterben abnehmen*).[5] In this sense, Being-toward-death designates an originary withdrawal to the hitherside of the being-with. In Being-in-the-world, it is the very that-which [*cela-même*] of *Dasein* that remains foreign to all others—which is not to say that Being-toward-death, as "authentic Being-toward-death," does not have as its initial effect that of enabling an altogether other being-with, an entirely different way of being-with-the-other in one and the same world: "Death is a possibility-of-being which *Dasein* itself has to take over in every case. With death, *Dasein* stands before itself in its ownmost potentiality-for-being. This is a possibility in which the issue is nothing less than *Dasein*'s Being-in-the-world. Its death is the possibility of no-longer being-able-to-be-there. If *Dasein* stands before itself as this possibility, it has been *fully* assigned to its ownmost potentiality-for-being. When it stands before itself in this way, all its relations to any other *Dasein* have been undone."[6]

Heidegger's analysis of "everydayness" provides a second reason why there are limits to our ability to share. Heidegger devotes almost all of sections 51 and 52 of *Being and Time*—titled, respectively, "Being-towards-Death and the Everydayness of *Dasein*," and "Everyday Being-towards-the-End and the Full Existential Conception of

Death"—to this analysis. Everything that can be made common and shared in the experience of death—everything, in this experience, that can be constitutive of a "we" (with one exception, to which we shall return)—is rejected in [*du côté de*] everydayness. The only thing that *Dasein* is in fact susceptible of sharing with others in its everyday relation to death is understood, in the terms of Heidegger's analysis, as the certainty that "we will all end up dying someday." To this a few strategies are added that enable us to live with this certainty. One might say that Heidegger undertakes a veritable *reduction* of this experience. He does so by articulating three modes that characterize our daily and *common* relation to death. The first, which he calls temptation (*Versuchung*), concerns the way in which the "they" speaks about death in general. It consists in digressing from the nature of the possibility, as possibility, that is "ownmost" to *Dasein*. It consists in covering up its absoluteness and insurpassibility [*indépassabilité*], in dissipating the relation of each of us to our end (the Being-toward-death, singular, of each *Dasein*) in some general statement, such as "one dies," "we die a little bit more every day," or "it happens all the time."

The second mode of sharing with others in our relation to death, considered generally, concerns our manner of addressing the dying. It belongs to everydayness because it is a form of propriety [*convenance*]. In addressing the dying, Heidegger explains, the "they" colludes [*s'entendrait*] in a general way to put off for as long as possible the instant at which *Dasein* is confronted with "his ownmost nonrelational possibility-of-being."[7] Confronted with the imminence of death, we have no alternative, no *shared* alternative, other than "a constant tranquilization about death"[8] (*eine ständige Beruhigung über den Tod*)—a tranquilization addressed as much to ourselves as to the person who is dying. We therefore collude *among ourselves* to persuade the one who is dying that his time has not yet come, that there will always be time to think about it—to provide comfort and solace, dodging the "Being authentically toward death" so as better to console—

and to bring comfort to ourselves at the same time. Finally there comes the last mode of this shared relation to death: the alienation of our anguish. In our common and everyday way of conducting ourselves in the face of death, everything conspires to turn death into a taboo. A code of good conduct is imposed. It consists of a twofold procedure: first, transforming anguish into fear of death; second, forbidding any expression of this fear, to the extent that it would amount to cowardice in the face of death and disturb the order of our preoccupations. Heidegger calls this third mode "alienation" (*Entfremdung*): "In addition, the anxiety which has been made ambiguous as fear, is passed off as a weakness with which no self-assured *Dasein* may have any acquaintance. What is 'fitting' according to the unuttered decree of the 'they,' is indifferent tranquility as to the 'fact' that one dies. The cultivation of such a 'superior' indifference *alienates Dasein* from its ownmost non-relational potentiality-for-being."[9]

Temptation (*Versuchung*), tranquilization (*Beruhigung*), and alienation (*Entfremdung*), according to *Being and Time*, are the three modes that everydayness provides us through which we share in our experience of death. We should retain three points from this analysis. First, there is the contrast between, on the one hand, *Dasein*'s relation with its ownmost possibility, which is a singular relationship (a withdrawal to the hitherside of [*en deçà de*] *Mitsein*) and, on the other hand, the different modes of the everyday relation to death, all common and shared, which reveal the idea that temptation, tranquilization, and alienation alone can be *shared*. Second, what Heidegger is describing as common and shared in our relation to death is placed entirely under the sign of the falling (*Verfallen*) of *Dasein*.[10] Everydayness therefore becomes the object of a generally (but not exclusively) negative assessment. Third, the narrowly construed alternatives in which the existential analytic of death is confined block any possibility (at least at this level of analysis) that the "thought of death" could accord with a "thought of the we." Heidegger's insistence on imputing these modes to the "they" confirms that temptation, tranquilization, and alienation are not constitutive of a "we." They create no bond. In the perspective of *Being and Time,* it is obviously inappropriate to speak of them as "sharing," as we have done up to this point for want of a better term.

Two questions emerge from these observations that will guide our analysis hereafter. The first consists in asking how, beyond *Being and Time,* the thought of Being-toward-death gives rise to thought of the "we." We shall see this juncture in Heidegger's commentaries on the hymns of Hölderlin, notably *Germania,* and, more specifically, in his thought on sacrifice. The second asks to what degree Heidegger's analytical framework reveals all there is that is common and shared in the relation to death. Can all shared experiences of death, all shared discourse, be tied, as Heidegger claims, to temptation, tranquilization, and alienation? The two questions come together in our concern to determine to what extent it might be the reduction (undertaken by the existential analytic of death) of all experience and of all common discourse to these three terms and to these three modes of falling that is compelling Heidegger to reflect on the political in terms of the sacrificial. Hence the corollary of this hypothetical interpretation, which we will address repeatedly in the following chapters: there can be no politics *other* (this *other* politics no doubt eluded Heidegger) than one grounded in a relation to death that is not one of temptation, tranquilization, or alienation—and as such is not alien to Being-toward-death—but a relation to death whose sharing is nonetheless not necessarily sacrificial, unless the "disposition toward sacrifice" were to assume a radically different meaning.[11]

In the various passages of *Being and Time* that we have examined so far there is an ever-present, underlying theme: that of language. Thinking the relation to death requires that we take into consideration the words that we address (or suppress) to one another about death or in the face of death—words that we hope or fear "to hear from one another" whenever one's experience is offered up for sharing. Such words are woven into our daily lives. They necessarily react to "news" of the passing of those who are both more or less close and familiar to us, but of those also who are foreign and far away. We hear talk of death and the dead through multiple channels, and we in turn talk of death and the dead ourselves. And yet, with a stroke of the pen, Heidegger crosses out all these words that compose our history (that of each of us singularly and that of all of us collectively) by systematically relegating them to idle talk. The only thing we know how to do about death, he tells us, is to talk about it idly and endlessly. Nothing illustrates better than these words the fact that, in everydayness, the relation we cultivate with death assumes the form of temptation, tranquilization, and alienation. The same is true of testimonies of death, and of equivocation, grief, and consternation at the death of another, of mourning and memory—none of which, by Heidegger's account, should require our attention or enter into our analysis. The analysis of Being-toward-death (which ties the relation to death to *Dasein*'s solitude) thus concludes, at the very moment at which it adumbrates the "existential projection of an authentic Being-toward-death," with the *interdiction* or *want* [*défaut*] of a hearing [*écoute*]. With respect to death, the analysis outlines that from which we have *nothing* to expect or to hear [*entendre*]. We shall return to this observation again and again.

Nevertheless, for all that, Heidegger does not conclude with this want, as we learn from the commentaries that, several years later, he will devote to the hymns, especially *Germania*, of Hölderlin.[12] These commentaries merit examination for at least two reasons. First, Heidegger's reading effectively fills this want, and in so doing suggests a second hypothesis, which would require extended scrutiny, notably regarding all that concerns the invocation of a "we" or an appeal to the German people. Second, it provides, in a decisive (penetrating, and not at all subsidiary) passage, a perfect symmetry with the paragraphs of *Being and Time* devoted to Being-toward-death, in effect taking up ideas developed in section 74, where Heidegger analyzes the place of death in the destiny of a community. The passage begins with Heidegger's reading of Hölderlin on "the nature of poetry as language," where he discusses the following verses:

> Since we are a dialogue
> And can hear from one another.[13]

By way of introduction, Heidegger reminds us that thinking of *Dasein* in its essence as dialogue requires that we consider dialogue simultaneously as poetry, silence, and idle talk. It is poetry to the extent that, called to account by the gods, we bring the existent to speech, we open it up to that which is, and at the same time we cover it with a veil. But it is also silence to the extent that the gods abandon us to ourselves, and their signs are wanting [*nous font défaut*]. It is idle talk, because we exhaust ourselves talking about things, according to the whimsy of our everyday preoccupations. To be dialogue is to hold fast to [*tenir*] that which makes language, as exposure to the Being of the existent, the most dangerous of all goods, while holding fast simultaneously to the risk that this exposure might degenerate into a simple discourse on things. Heidegger, with this understanding, then tries to comprehend this mutual understanding, evoked by Hölderlin's second verse, by dissociating it from any exchange of communication. To understand one another is to share the exposure that is dialogue—a sharing that brings us back to the most originary community, to the community that precedes this mutual understanding and makes it possible. Hence the question becomes: What do we share, what do we have in common that allows *us* to understand one another? What is common to us, prior to the very possibility of silence as to that of idle talk, that makes community possible? Where does this "we" come from such that it is prior to all possible "they's" [*on*].

This is where the commentary on Hölderlin intersects the analysis of Being-toward-death. It intersects it, reprises the terms, but takes an additional step. To accede to this originary community, Heidegger explains, one must follow the thread that leads to the prohibition of any retreat [*repli*] by this community back toward a society whose meaning is the sharing of some or other everyday preoccupation. This originary community, if it exists, must engage each *Dasein* with that which is its ownmost—that which Heidegger characterizes as "*each individual* being bound in advance to something that binds and determines every individual in exceeding them."[14] The primordial bond, in other words, is that which binds each and every one (and which determines *Dasein* in totality) to that which is its ownmost, and yet which is common to all, not in the sense that it is the same for all, but in the sense that everyone shares, *in common,* in having this bond as his ownmost [*auraient en commun de l'avoir en propre*]. But that which each *Dasein* has as its ownmost, its ownmost possibility—we know from *Being and Time*—is Being-toward-death. And yet it is this possibility that confines *Dasein* in solitude [*esseule*]. Heidegger reprises this claim, in the same terms, in his commentary on Hölderlin. Now, however, this solitude becomes something that is shared—but shared in very specific circumstances (described as exemplary), which are undeniably political, that is to say the circumstances of a shared sacrifice for the fatherland. This passage merits a lengthy quotation:

> The comradeship of soldiers on the front is based neither on the fact that people had to join together because other human beings, from whom one was removed, were absent; nor did it have its basis in people first agreeing to a shared enthusiasm; rather, its most profound and sole basis lies in the fact that the nearness of death as a sacrifice placed everyone in advance into the same nothingness, so that the latter became the source of an unconditional belonging to

one another. Precisely death, which each individual human being must die for him- or herself, and which individuates each individual upon themselves to the most extreme degree, precisely death and the readiness for its sacrifice first of all creates in advance the space of that community out of which comradeship emerges. Then comradeship springs from anxiety? No and yes. No, if like a petit bourgeois one understands anxiety as merely a helpless wavering in a panic-stricken state of cowardliness. Yes, if anxiety is conceived as the metaphysical proximity to what is unconditional, a proximity bestowed only to a supreme steadfastness and readiness. If we fail to compel into our *Dasein* powers that bind and individuate just as unconditionally as death as free sacrifice, that is, powers that attack at the roots of the *Dasein* of each individual, and that stand just as profoundly and entirely within a genuine knowing, then no "comradeship" will emerge; at most, we shall attain an altered form of society.[15]

Heidegger had already explained in *Being and Time* that *Dasein*'s way of being-with with others in the same world (which *Dasein* can never abandon) would be radically modified if *Dasein* could be torn away [*arraché*] from the "they" and could reappropriate its ownmost possibility—if, in other words, *Dasein* could achieve, in solitude, an "authentic Being-toward-death." Such a modification could arise from *Dasein*'s disposition toward a "freely consented sacrifice" (which is for *Dasein* the reappropriation of its ownmost possibility). At this point at which the disposition toward sacrifice restores *Dasein* to what is most unique to *Dasein,* this same disposition would exclude, Heidegger explains, any corrupt relation toward the existence of the other, any misunderstanding of the possibilities of the other's existence, and any temptation to fold these other possibilities of existence into *Dasein*'s own. Already in *Being and Time,* the reconciliation between *Dasein*'s disposition toward the extreme possibility that is self-sacrifice and its determination as being-with "who has some understanding of the potentiality-for-being of others"—"Mitsein verstehend für das Seinkönnen der Anderen"—is already clear. Heidegger's commentary on the hymns of Hölderlin will return to this reconciliation using different terms "Anticipation discloses to existence that its uttermost possibility lies in giving itself up, and thus it shatters all one's tenaciousness to whatever existence one has reached. . . . As the non-relational possibility, death individualizes—but only in such a manner that, as the possibility which is not to be out-stripped, it makes *Dasein,* as being-with, have some understanding of the potentiality-for-being of others."[16]

In the passage taken from the commentary on *Germania,* cited above, this reconciliation is made even more imperative and its political resonance more immediate—especially when we recall what this commentary constructs regarding the concept of the people and the first person plural.[17] What the commentary brings explicitly into relation is, in effect, "nearness of death as a sacrifice" and "unconditional belonging to one another." As always with Heidegger, this relationship supposes that other ways of understanding this belonging are forcefully cast aside. Belonging, he says, cannot be sought in the enthusiasm of the warrior (i.e., in the intoxication of sharing in combat), nor in the distress of separation, but rather only in the proximity, indeed the imminence of death. We could make three observations. First, this passage no doubt reflects the intellectual and moral climate of the interwar period in Germany, as reconstructed, for example, by Domenico Losurdo in *Heidegger and the Ideology of War.* Its ideology, we should recall, is distinctive not only by its invocation of the community (which we find again in Heidegger's Rectoral Address), but also by its critique of any idealization of security (which is one of the analytical themes of Being-toward-death in its relation to everydayness). But beyond the historical context (which, we should note, neither Karl Jaspers nor Max Weber were able to escape), we ought also to interrogate the nature of the experience of "camaraderie" that is being evoked, and of the narrative that is conveying it. *Being and Time* rejects all scientific approaches to death as inadequate to *Dasein*'s authentic relation to its ownmost possibility. Similarly, in his commentary on Hölderlin, Heidegger invokes not scientific knowledge but rather a shared experience—that of the proximity of death on the front lines—that we can know only through the narratives that are handed down to us. Heidegger cannot derive the experience of camaraderie in the trenches from logic. He can only interpret the narratives that have been written about them. He is therefore obliged to rely on such narratives and on their capacity to transmit the experience in question, which is to say, on their adequation to something like an experience of a sacrificial community as it faces death. Recalling what Walter Benjamin wrote regarding the poverty of experience, we might ask if such an experience and its narration are possible. Where does Heidegger get the idea that acquiescence in common sacrifice effectively constitutes the essence of what soldiers are sharing on the front lines? How does he draw the survivors out of their silence?[18] A second remark regarding this short passage points in the same direction. Granting the notion of sacrifice, for the sake of argument, it nevertheless assumes something more than an "authentic Being-toward-death." It assumes in effect that those who died on the front lines did not die in vain, without reason, and that their death was not absurd. Otherwise, we would expect to hear of revolts against such sacrifice, of refusals to die for nothing. But to speak of sacrifice as Heidegger does is, to the contrary, to refer back at least implicitly to a "for what" (for the fatherland, for liberty, for honor, for the people . . .) that exceeds "authentic Being-toward-death" in the strict sense of the term. This is what Heidegger in fact does in his May 1933 speech in homage to Albert Leo Schlageter.[19] The shared sacrifice, as a sharing, must therefore refer to a shared theme that Heidegger chose not to develop in his commentary. The third and final point follows from the first two and enables us to conclude. What Heidegger seems to assume is that, in the end, in the trenches, the shared relation to death could not be thought otherwise than as a shared acceptance [*consentement*] of sacrifice. This is to say that, in the face of imminent death, there is no other way to unite *against* [*faire front contre*] death than through this acceptance. And yet we encounter narratives of the "camaraderie of the trenches," to use Heidegger's expression (*die Kameradschaft der Frontsoldaten*), as emblematic form and revelation of the community to itself, which show a very different relation to death. They show a relation that consists specifically in coming together to oppose death with the greatest possible resistance, to effectively join forces against it (against hunger, against the cold, against illness, but also against enemy fire) through mutual assistance. One might call this relation "being-against-death."[20]

"Being-against-death" is neither the refusal of death nor the attempt to escape death, nor is it the "hysterical trembling of a cowardice that has lost its head" that Heidegger lampoons again and again with disconcerting facility. Nor does it exclude an "authentic Being-toward-death," though it might radically transform its meaning. Nevertheless, this "being-against-death" could well open up the possibility for a very different kind of politics—a politics freed from the sacrificial. But Heidegger's cursory allusion to the camaraderie of the trenches, by way of his commentary on Hölderlin, is silent on such a possibility. It may also be what is lacking in his analysis of Being-toward-death in *Being and Time,* and it is perhaps because of that lack that Heidegger's analysis, with untold results, forecloses the political.

Surprising in this analysis is the fact that the evocation of war (World War I) is so fleeting, and the recollection of its destructiveness so succinct. They only inspire the author of *Being and Time* with thoughts of acceptance of sacrifice—as if sacrifice were all that the horror of war had to teach us about "sharing death." The expression "Being-against-death" seeks to give grounds [*faire droit*] for a different memory of war, conjointly and inseparably with a different relation to death—one that both evokes and connotes resistance and a common front, as well as something like the proximity of risk and danger, perhaps even a multiplicity of shared dangers. Thinking along these lines obviously raises two objections that must be examined. The first is that such a front belongs entirely to the "experienceability of the death of an other," the pertinence of which Heidegger denies. The second is that such a front is simply a variation on the falling of *Dasein* into everydayness, a falling that is the corollary of temptation, tranquilization, and alienation.

What specifically, then, does this "Being-against-death" denote? First and foremost, it is a kind of "being-one-for-another" in opposing death, in uniting against it, in suffering its proximity collectively. For this reason it is not about my own death exclusively nor about that of others independently of my own, but about a mutual need that ties us to one another in the singular relation that we each have toward our ownmost possibility (the possibility of our impossibility), a need to hold off the day of reckoning—which also means to prevent that one or the other of us hastens or precipitates that day.[21] In considering "being-with-one-another," which denotes an essential structure of the constitution of *Dasein*, such a front (against my death as well as against that of any other) requires that we take into account, as constitutive, *the primary possibility* (here and elsewhere) of a misfortune that leads to the brink of death, as well as to famine, to disease, to the unavailability of assistance (and to the inequalities that accompany such unavailability), to murder and all forms of violent death—as well as to the means to resist this possibility, as shared means. This does not imply, on the part of each *Dasein*, any temptation to deny or to flee Being-toward-death. Nor does it suggest tranquilization or consolation. On the contrary, to form a front against death is to confront death without resigning oneself to letting death come without resistance. For this reason, neither can being-against-death be understood as alienation. In other words, if, in the relation to death, everydayness is dominated by the opinion that death strikes the "they" first ("they" die), and if, as Heidegger writes, everydayness downgrades death to an event that does not properly strike anyone, then death in everydayness is quite the opposite of what is being played out in the shared "being-against-death." The latter deals *only with singular deaths*. It resists death only because death can in fact strike each *Dasein* as singularity—that is to say, that death is for each and everyone his ownmost possibility.

In sum, "being-against-death" does not dispossess *Dasein* of its singular Being-toward-death. Being-toward-death happens only to be *recognized* [*accordée*] in the others. The issue is how it is being recognized. Nothing can be taken for granted. Some ways of recognizing Being-toward-death in others can be disastrous, and give rise to all sorts of exclusivist [*sécuritaires*], authoritarian, and totalitarian policies. But it is precisely because of the possibility and the danger of such policies (which Heidegger never understood, anticipated, or denounced) that we must refer back to the being-against-death that inspires them. Such policies must be thought from the vantage point of being-against-death so as to be more effectively opposed and combated. Politics cannot be thought independently of these modes of recognition. It may even be the case that all politics (the "best" as well as the "worst") has its origin in the conversion of the *Being-toward-death* of *a multiplicity* of singularities into a *being-against-death* that is shared. Might this not be the path that Sartre, Levinas, Patočka, Ricœur, Derrida, and others explored? Is this why they all assume the difficult inheritance of Heidegger's text, which they will read, meditate, and critique under the cloud of war in the twentieth century?

2

Dying-for

⇒ JEAN-PAUL SARTRE ⇐

Few passages of Sartre's architecturally complex work *Being and Nothingness* are more critical of the existential analytic of *Being and Time* than those, in the fourth and last part, devoted to "*my* death." Heidegger's summons to an authentic Being-toward-death—to the acknowledgment by *Dasein* that death is its ownmost possibility—becomes, translated into Sartre's idiom, the realization of a "project toward death," the realization of a "freedom-to-die" that allows *Dasein* to "constitute itself as totality by [its] free choice of finitude."[1] The idea that death can be the object of such a project [*projet*] is thus, from the beginning, put in question in a radical way. But death is not merely one theme among others in Sartre's essay on phenomenological ontology, published in 1943 (the date is important). The question whether death can be "recovered [*recupéré*] by freedom"[2] makes an appearance in nearly all the theatrical works that Sartre wrote in the following decade, beginning with *The Flies, The Victors, Dirty Hands,* and of course *No Exit.* Indeed, a close reading of these plays reveals that each presents, successively, a mise-en-scène of an argument that Sartre developed in *Being and Nothingness* in critical engagement with Heidegger's analysis of Being-toward-death. Nevertheless, these plays cannot simply be reduced to such arguments. *The Victors, Dirty Hands,* and *The Condemned of Altona* evoke death only to the extent that it participates in an "engagement" with history or politics.

Does this not mean, however, that it is this possibility of engagement, as possibility, that is in play in the thought of death? Is this the meaning of Sartre's complaint regarding Heidegger's "sleight of hand" [*tour de passe passe*]—a sleight of hand that *Being and Nothingness* dissects with great precision,[3] and against which Sartre's theatrical compositions expose, with equal force, other possibilities?

If Sartre is able to pursue this dissection through different literary genres, it is because the organizing thread that guides it evinces a clear dramatic tension. The concept with which Sartre will, in page after page (and play after play), oppose the considerable privilege accorded by Heidegger to Being-toward-death, is in effect nothing less than the *absurdity* of death:

> What must be noted first is the absurd character of death. In this sense every attempt to consider it as a resolved chord at the end of a melody must be sternly rejected. It has often been said that we are in the situation of a condemned man among other condemned men who is ignorant of the day of his execution but who sees each day that his fellow prisoners are being executed. This is not wholly exact. We ought rather to compare ourselves to a man condemned to death who is bravely preparing himself for the ultimate penalty, who is doing everything possible to make a good showing on the scaffold, and who meanwhile is carried off by a flu epidemic.[4]

What makes death absurd? Heidegger's enterprise, Sartre explains, involves two steps. The first is to individualize death—that is, Heidegger reminds us that my death is the only thing that belongs to me alone. It is because of this that the individuation of *Dasein* itself becomes possible. If no one can die in *Dasein*'s place, *Dasein* achieves an authentic existence by projecting itself toward this ultimate possibility. "Being-toward-death," therefore, should be conceived as that which enables *Dasein* to perceive itself as an irreplaceable totality.

Dasein will be this totality to the extent (and only to the extent) that *its* death will belong to it. But, we ask, is such an *appropriation* possible? This is what Sartre seeks to put in doubt by asking, by way of introduction and before fully developing his critique of Heidegger's thought on death, "But is the death which will overtake me *my* death?"[5]

There is no doubt that we can take issue here and there with the terms that the author of *Being and Nothingness* uses to translate Heidegger's language—Heidegger did so himself. The fact nevertheless remains that Heidegger considers the appropriation of death to be the key to authenticity. And in so doing he bars from consideration [*fait l'impasse*] all the ways we might conceptualize a "dispossession of death" (my death is not *my* death) that would confer on death an entirely different meaning. What are these ways? How do they controvert the existential analytic? *Being and Nothingness* will develop at length possible representations of such a dispossession. As for Sartre's theatrical works, they will put these representations on stage. *No Exit, The Victors,* and *Dirty Hands* all participate in the staging of various configurations of just such a *dispossession*.

Three steps can be distinguished in Sartre's dismantling of Being-toward-death and of the ontological privilege that is attached to it. The first step is to question the exclusivity of such a privilege. To what extent, Sartre asks, can one maintain that death is the only one of my possibilities that is absolutely mine alone? It is true that no one can *die* in my place, but we could also argue that no one can *love* in my place. The love that I feel for someone cannot be delegated. Or, more accurately, it cannot be delegated unless considered from a functional point of view—that is to say, independently of my subjectivity. If to love means "to make someone happy," nothing says that I am the only one who can do so. It is therefore not love, as such, that is irreplaceable, but rather the *situation* that defines it. The same applies to death (*my* death). There are hypothetical situations in which death can also be reduced to a function that dispossesses *me* of *my* death. In the case of *dying for* the fatherland, or for some other cause, it is this cause that gives death its significance rather than the fact that it is *me* (and no one else) who dies. Anyone can die for the fatherland in my place, as shown by a gloomy litany of wars, martyrdoms, and victims—unless, that is, we were to refer this "dying for" to the free and responsible choice that alone could give it meaning, and unless we were to suppose (but this is less than obvious) that this choice could be effectively honored:

> If to die is to die in order to inspire, to bear witness, for the country, etc., then anybody at all can die in my place—as in the song in which lots are drawn to see who is to be eaten. In short there is no personalizing virtue which is peculiar to *my* death. Quite the contrary, it becomes *my* death only if I place myself already in the perspective of subjectivity; it is my subjectivity defined by the pre-reflective *cogito* which makes of my death a subjective irreplaceable [*un irremplaçable subjectif*], and not death which would give an irreplaceable selfness to my for-itself. In this case death cannot be characterized; for it is *death* as *my* death, and consequently its essential structure as death is not sufficient to make of it that personalized and qualified event which one can *wait* for.[6]

It is worth our while, for at least two reasons, to spend some time examining the structure of this "dying for." First, though it comes up in a digression that looks like a mere cavil, it decisively overturns the problematic of *Being and Time*. Or, more accurately, it exposes what is *lacking* in the existential analytic. We can envisage the possibility of our own death in many ways, but these various ways do not endow this possibility with the same meaning. One can die of old age in one's bed. One can be struck down in one's prime by sickness or accident, or blown away by the whirlwinds of history, war, and revolution. Or, finally, one can die in the service of a cause that one chooses to defend *unto death*. Supposing, then, that I take each of these possibilities under consideration as to the death that might befall me, I do not project myself at death in the same way. They do not give the same meaning to what would be *my* death. To think on death as the ineluctable end of a long life is to acknowledge and accept that my life as a whole has an end. Inversely, imagining that a sudden illness or accident might carry me away comes down to realizing the possibility that, on the contrary, my life might be brutally interrupted—that, for reasons of contingency that do not depend on me, the projects that are mine, the possibilities that are offered to me, might be *prematurely* shattered.

But of all these possibilities it is that of *dying for* that displaces, in a most significant way, the problematic of *Being and Time*. By considering the possibility of *dying for* some or other cause, Sartre restores a political dimension to our relation to death. Indeed, if there is one (political) question that characterizes the last century, it is not so much the question of knowing to what extent an authentic Being-toward-death enables us to avoid foundering in the everydayness than it is the question of knowing the *for what* of death—not the *for what* of sacrifice in general, but of *that* for which it might be worthwhile to be sacrificed. If it is true that the expressions "to die *for* the fatherland," "to die *for* liberty," "to die *for* truth," "to die *for* another" all point to the problematic character of the relation to death, they are all nevertheless only saying this: it is not the possibility of my death as arguably my ownmost possibility (which makes my death *my* death), but rather that for which I decide that I could die (assuming, again, that such a decision is possible) that gives meaning to my existence.

This is the question, as we know, that haunted every movement of resistance, every sedition [*dissidences*], revolt, revolution, and, no doubt, every political combat of the past century. It is therefore not surprising to hear it expressed repeatedly by some of the most significant heroes of Sartre's plays. In *The Flies,* written and produced the year that *Being and Nothingness* was published, Orestes's tutor describes the inhabitants of Argos—a country under foreign occupation—as "perishing of fear"[7]—that is, as men and women obstructed by terror from projecting any possibility of dying *for* liberty or *for* truth. Inversely, it is *for* these two causes (so as to purify the city of falsehood and fear) that Orestes, at the peril of his life, risks the furor of the Erinyes and the anger of the crowd. In *The Victors* (1946), which narrates the stay of execution of captives who are condemned to death and tortured, both the relations between the victims and their "dialogue" with their executioners disclose the tense need to wrestle, throughout the play, with the burdensome question, "To die for what?" Henri, one of the imprisoned resistance fighters, declares in Act I:

> You lived for the cause, yes. But don't try to tell me that it's for the cause you are going to die. Perhaps if we had succeeded and died in action, then perhaps—[a pause]. We shall die because we were given an idiotic assignment and because we executed it badly. Our death serves no one. The cause didn't need to have this village attacked. . . . We tried to justify our lives and we missed out. Now we are going to die. We'll be dead and will be unjustified corpses.[8]

The torment experienced by Garcin, one of the three protagonists of *No Exit,* is largely induced by his inability to know whether he died as a hero, for liberty and for truth, or as a coward because he deserted in the face of the enemy. He is exposed, even in his relations with others and despite all his demands, to the undecidability of *dying for*—an undecidability that does not allow him to "possess" his own death, and thus prohibits him from being assured that his death is in fact *his* death and serves to give meaning to his existence. *Dirty*

Hands, undoubtedly the most important play in this context, circles relentlessly around the question of the "*for what* of death" and finds in it the path toward its denouement. If Hugo makes the personal decision to open the door to killers who lie in wait, it is because this fatal action enables Hœderer, whom he himself had assassinated four years earlier, not to have died *for nothing.* It is by his own death that he seeks to preserve the meaning of the death of his own victim. The play thus culminates in the splitting and mirroring [*dédoublement*] of "dying for": that of the death of Hœderer and that of the death of Hugo. At the same time it reveals—as do *No Exit* and *The Victors*—that "dying for" is, in the end, always contingent on the regard of the other. It is up to Hugo, as long as he still lives, to decide for what Hœderer has died. And yet the meaning that this decision gives to the death of his victim, as well as to his own death as he projects it, only lasts as long as he lives. As soon as it is carried out, the meaning of his act (and with it the meaning of his entire life) no longer belongs to him. It falls (with the curtain) under the sway of the commentaries of others (Louis, Olga, and the others), just as, in *No Exit,* Garcin, Estelle, and Inès hear friends, acquaintances, and colleagues from their past determine the meaning of their death and, with it, the meaning of their existence. Thus whatever meaning he gave to his own death (as totalization of his existence), the "hero" of *Dirty Hands,* once dead, is himself dispossessed of it. Death, given over to the regard of others, strips away all assurance concerning the *for what* of "dying for":

> HUGO [not taking the gun]: You have made Hœderer a great man. But
>   I loved him more than you could ever love him. If I renounced
>   my deed he would become a nameless corpse, a throw-off of the
>   party. [The car stops.] Killed by accident. Killed over a woman.
> OLGA: Get out of here.
> HUGO: A man like Hœderer doesn't die by accident. He dies for his
>   ideas, for his political program; he's responsible for his death. If

I openly claim my crime and declare myself Raskolnikov and am willing to pay the necessary price, then he will have the death he deserves.[9]

Such is Sartre's first move in his critique of the existential analytic of death. The problematic of the authentic or inauthentic character of Being-toward-death slips into that of the undecidability of *dying for*. Can I ever know what I would be ready to die for? And, if I do not know, who will? Even if I am ready to die for some cause, will *my* death be redeemed by my freedom? In this undecidability the absurd nature of death is foreshadowed—all the more so given that *dying for* is also disclosing something else. In Sartre's plays, the characters never die of old age. No matter what the *for what* of their death, death interrupts their existence with brutality. The deaths of Hugo and Hœderer in *Dirty Hands,* those of François, Sorbier, Henri, Lucie, and Canoris in *The Victors,* that of Garcin (and even Estelle and Inès) in *No Exit,* do not totalize their existence. They bring it to an end, but leave it unfinished [*elles l'inachèvent en l'achevant*]. For all these characters, to think of death (whether imminent or past) is not to think on a possibility that gives meaning to all other possibilities, to the extent that it is one's ownmost, but rather on the contingent, brutally imposed impossibility of further projecting the meaning of their lives. Such is the unendurable distress of the characters of *No Exit.* The meaning of their existence no longer belongs to them. It is no longer in their power to project a *modification* of that meaning. Such is also the fear of the characters of the other plays. *Dying for* [*mourir pour*] therefore has no meaning other than that of struggling to one's last breath to vanquish the absurdity of this interruption. *Dying because of* [*mourir par*] opposition to the lies and the shame [*compromissions*], like Hugo, or heroically as a martyr (for truth and liberty), defying torture, like the heroes of *The Victors,* is to struggle, by a death that is *qualified,* to escape a death that is meaningless. In their cell, Canoris, Sorbier, Henri, or Lucie do not so much fear execution as the prospect of seeing the meaning of their lives definitively (irredeemably) compromised if they confess and talk before dying.[10]

If, therefore, *dying for* overturns the signification of Being-toward-death, it is to the extent that the death that it thematizes never remains indeterminate. The death of *dying for* is a *qualified* death. And it is only by virtue of this qualification that *dying for* can hope to redeem both death and existence from absurdity. Thus it is no accident that in the most decisive move of Sartre's critique of Heidegger in *Being and Nothingness,* this same *dying for* is set aside as a possible exception to this absurdity:

> What then could be the meaning of a waiting for death if it is not the waiting for an undetermined event which would reduce all waiting to the absurd, even including that of death itself? A waiting for death would be self-destructive, for it would be the negation of all waiting. My project toward a particular death is comprehensible (suicide, martyrdom, heroism) but not the project toward *my* death as the undetermined possibility of no longer realizing a presence in the world, for this project would be the destruction of all projects. Thus death cannot be my peculiar possibility; it cannot even be one of *my* possibilities.[11]

With regard to this *dying for,* as faintly suggested here by the inter-related representations [*figures*] of martyrdom and heroism, Sartre says only that it is comprehensible. But it is comprehensible in the same way as are the "situations" in which his dramatic characters relate to (*their?*) death. They relate to death in a way that makes no distinction between authenticity and inauthenticity, but rather as a way of offering the possibility of endowing existence with meaning. It is "comprehensible," but does it in fact void [*ôter*] death's absurdity? In other words, does "dying for" enable a "reappropriation" of

death? We noted above that Sartre's critique of the existential analytic of Being-toward-death was articulated around three moves. The
first consisted in denouncing the privilege accorded to *my* death, as
the possibility that is *my* ownmost. The second revealed the absurdity of death as the irreversible suspension of the meaning of life. Both
these moves, with respect to Heidegger's analyses, tend to present
death as a contingent event that could in no way serve as the object
of an *appropriation*. They reveal that my death is never *my* death—
never *my* possibility. Far from belonging to me, it dispossesses me of
myself. Nevertheless, the possibility remains, despite everything, that
death might still be redeemed by freedom on condition that it be
"qualified"—on condition, that is, that I do not die for nothing, but
for a cause: liberty, truth, justice, and so forth. It is this possibility
that drives the dramatic narrative of several of the plays Sartre wrote
in the aftermath of his essay on fundamental ontology. In *Being and
Nothingness,* however, it is barely adumbrated.

The possibility of *dying for* is barely adumbrated because anything in
the analysis that might look like a hope for "redemption" [*salut*] is
quashed by the analysis' third move. Even if the temptation of "dying
for" is comprehensible, it nevertheless does not bring "redemption"
from the absurdity of death. For if death must be thought in terms of
absurdity, it is not only because it leaves the meaning of my existence
in suspense. It is (and perhaps primarily) because it abandons the
totality of my existence to the judgment of others. It is an illusion to
think that with (my) death my existence sees its meaning established
and thus "justified." In reality, the "justification" that would *redeem*
me does not belong to *me*. It is not in my power to "give" this justification in relating in such and such way to (my) life and to its end. On
the contrary, if every death is absurd, it is first and foremost because
no death escapes the law that makes of others the depositories of its

hypothetical *justification*. This explains the distress of Garcin, Estelle, and Inès in *No Exit,* who, as we saw above, are attentive from beyond the grave to what others say about them, to the utterances they hear, for a time, like a faraway murmur, which they are powerless to correct or shape:

> GARCIN: There they are, slumped in their chairs sucking at their cigars. Bored they look. Half-asleep. They're thinking: "Garcin's a coward." But only vaguely, dreamily. One's got to think of something. "That chap Garcin was a coward." That's what they've decided, those dear friends of mine. In six month's time they'll be saying: "Cowardly as that skunk Garcin." You're lucky, you two; no one on earth is giving you another thought. But I—I'm long in dying.[12]

Cowardice! Sartre develops this same example of cowardice, significantly in 1943 in *Being and Nothingness,* as he holds exposure to the judgment and memory of others to be the "characteristic of a dead life": "We can go on to qualify a particular episode as 'cowardly' or 'tactless' without, however, ever losing sight of the fact that only the contingent arrest of this 'being-in-perpetual-suspense' which is the living for-itself allows us on the foundation of a radical absurdity to confer a relative meaning on the episode considered, and that this meaning is an *essentially provisory* meaning, the provisory quality of which has *accidentally passed* into the definitive."[13]

He will dwell longer on this point in *Being and Death.* It is in fact Sartre's most decisive critique of sections 46–53 of *Being and Time,* and its importance is considerable. As we saw above, Heidegger's analysis only holds to the extent that *Dasein*'s relation to its ownmost possibility radically confines *Dasein* to solitude [*esseule*]. Although it is true that every *Dasein* (being there) is *Mitsein mit der anderen* (being-with with others), the projection of an authentic Being-toward-death assumes, inversely, the suspension of any relation between *Dasein* and others. The regard, the judgments, the opinions of others, Heidegger tells us, cannot intervene in the way in which I relate to my own death. This means that any consideration of my survival in the memory of others will have to be set aside as inauthentic. In relating to my own death I therefore forego considering the memory that others (beginning with those closest to me) will retain of me.

Sartre, by turning death into "the triumph of the other's point of view," undertakes to overturn Heidegger's entire framework [*dispositif*]. Death's triumph does not simply gesture toward absurdity. It also means, just as essentially, that I, while living, deal more with the deaths of others than I do with my own—not simply in the sense that I am afflicted by *their* death, but in the sense that *their* death turns me into the custodian [*gardien*] of *their* past life. Death, to the extent that it is the annihilation of my possibilities, positions my being as in-itself [*est position de mon être comme en-soi*]. My life, as it ceases to be "its own suspense"[14] [*sursis*, postponement or stay of execution], exists no longer except in the memory of others. To think on one's death is not to try to appropriate it so as to make of it one's ownmost possibility, but to project in the future an ineluctable alienation. My death, far from belonging to me alone—such that I can, in projecting it, perceive myself as totality—turns my life into the possession of another. It is an open-ended totality whose meaning, in the last resort, does not belong to me. In the end, nothing that I shall have done, nothing that I shall have been, not one of my words, and not a single one of my acts, will belong to me any longer as my ownmost—*assuming that they ever did*. And because I anticipate this alienation while I still live, and because I grow concerned about the memory of me that those near and not so near to me will retain, and of the meaning that they will attribute to my undertakings, it is while I still live that I try (as if better to expunge [*conjurer*] death's absurd character) to pre-orient or to pre-determine the meaning that will be given to my life and my works: "To be dead is to be a prey for the living. This means therefore that the one who tries to grasp the meaning of his future death must discover himself as the future prey of others."[15]

And yet, if it is true that my death does not belong to me, it is also true—in ways that remain to be examined—that the deaths of others do belong to me. It is up to me to decide whether *their* past lives will be forgotten, or whether I will remember them and, if so, how I will remember them. Death, therefore, does not confine me to solitude. I am bound to others by the conscience that I have of death's absurd character, both unappropriated [*inapproprié*] and incapable of appropriation, and of the abyss that it cleaves, not between me and others, but between me and myself. This is, in the end, how *Being and Nothingness* overturns *Being and Time*. For Heidegger, I cannot define myself otherwise than by the relation that I maintain with the possibility of my own death. It is in the projection of an authentic Being-toward-death that I fully "belong to myself." Any relation to the death of others falls under the heading of everydayness and the dominion of the "they." For Sartre, on the contrary, the relation to the death of others brings me back to death's absurd character—however much I try to escape it. Even when violence, oppression, injustice, and misery enable me to project my death in the mode of "dying for," death still is not redemption. Even if I should try to *reappropriate* it, it will never be anything other than "a certain aspect of facticity and of being-for-others—i.e., nothing other than the given."[16] And yet it is not foreign to my freedom and my responsibility. The inverse of this disappropriation (i.e., the acknowledgment of death's absurdity), Sartre writes in a decisive passage, is the "whole of my responsibility toward the dead":

> In reality the relation with the dead—with *all* the dead—is an essential structure of the fundamental relations which we have called "being-for-others." In its upsurge into being, the for-itself must assume a position in relation to the dead. . . . It is not impossible (provided

one understands this properly) to define a "person" by his dead—
i.e., by the areas of individualization or of collectivization which he
has determined in the necropolis, by the roads and pathways which
he has traced, by the information which he has decided to get for himself, by the "roots" which he has put down there. Of course the dead
choose us, but it is necessary first that we have chosen them. We
find here again the original relation which binds facticity to freedom:
we choose our own attitude toward the dead, but it is not possible
for us not to choose an attitude. . . . Thus by its very facticity, the for-
itself is thrown into full "responsibility" with respect to the dead; it
is obliged to decide freely the fate of the dead.[17]

Here the relation to death assumes an altogether different dimension, inviting several observations. If it is true, first of all, that our existence is a fabric of relations—what Sartre calls "being-for-others"—
this fabric is not composed of relations with living beings alone, but
also with the dead and even with *all* the dead. It is not merely a question of beings we have known, of friends and family whom we mourn
when they pass away. "*All* the dead"[18] means that my life *with* the
dead extends beyond the set of those on whom I can place a name
and a face. However, they do not *all* belong to my existence equally;
I do not accord them the same survival [*la même survie*]; I do not feel
the same responsibility toward them. In the immense necropolis that
is human history the dead endure individually (when their name
and their works survive them), or as constitutive but undifferenti-
ated elements of anonymous masses of various magnitudes. It thus
belongs to me to choose the dead with whom I will *make* my life: the
writers I will read, the artists whose works I shall admire, as well as
the "peoples," the "communities," the "movements," and the "assem-
blies" of people whose actions will retain my attention.

This election of the dead—and of the relation that *I* will have to
maintain with them—is not limited to a knowledge of history. It is

an integral part of my Being-for-myself. In making myself, in one way or another, the custodian of these former lives—in not allowing some one or other of these lives to "shrivel up in its plenitude in-itself by cutting all its moorings with the present"[19]—I project myself into the future. In the memories that I retain of some one or other, individually or collectively, I am not merely responsible for their survival. I am, first and foremost, responsible for the Being that I choose, with them, to become. Doubtless, death cannot be redeemed [*récupéré*] by freedom. But freedom needs the dead. It needs to decide with whom among the dead it wants to *live*. I alone can make this decision. True, it can be imposed on me (by education, by the society in which I live, by a political regime)—but in this case I must choose to submit or resist [*contredire*]. I must say whether the *dead* of my family, like those of the state, those that they honor and commemorate, whose names they invoke and to whose memory they raise statues, are also *my* dead.

This amounts to saying that such an election from among the dead is always a political one. The remembrance I retain of history's victims, of oppressed peoples, of the "just" and the "heroes," of tyrants and persecutors—of those dead whom I choose not to forget—engages me politically. I can still envisage the possibility of "dying for," but it will not redeem me [*sauvera*]. My task, however, in the life that I project, is to remember (or not to remember) those who did "die for": for freedom, for truth, for justice, for others, for nothing. To live is always *to live with*. The life that I project is a life that is shared. And from the moment that the memory of the dead belongs to my project, it is also that which divides what is shared. The multiple relations that I maintain with others are affected, *in diverse ways,* by the way that they and I relate *ourselves* to the dead. My memory of the dead brings me close to some and separates me from others. Beyond the relation *with all the dead*, it is therefore my relation with my contemporaries—*all the living*—that this memory affects. My life is a fabric of relations with others both dead and living. It is the evolving and irreplaceable singularity of this fabric (and not an authentic Being-toward-death) that is mine. No one is an exception. Each of us is made up from all of humanity, living and dead—and no projection of one's own death in isolation will deliver us from the constitutive relation that binds us to all humanity. Sartre reminds us of this in the concluding words of his autobiography: "If I relegate impossible Salvation to the prop room, what remains? A whole man, composed of all men and as good as all of them and no better than any."[20]

3

Vanquishing Death

⇒ EMMANUEL LEVINAS ⇐

Before a pure event, a future event, which is death, where the ego
can in no way be able—that is, can no longer be an ego—I seek a
situation where nonetheless it is possible for it to remain an ego,
and I have called this situation "victory over death."

—EMMANUEL LEVINAS, *Time and the Other*

As stated in the introduction, none of the philosophical engagements
with Heidegger's *Being and Time* in the last century is more clearly
marked by the memory of World War II—by the torment of mass murder, the assassinations, the untold executions, and, most extraordinar-
ily, the deportation and extermination of the Jews of Europe, which
distinguishes this war from all others—than the thought of Emmanuel
Levinas. It is this torment that makes for the uniqueness of the thought
of death that Levinas elaborates in the pages of his work. It keeps
alive, like no other, the memory of the victims of hatred, of each victim singularly and irreducibly. Levinas dedicates his work to their
memory and to the justice that is their due, as stated explicitly in the
dedication of *Otherwise Than Being; or, Beyond Essence,* published in
1974: "To the memory of those who were closest among the six mil-
lion who were assassinated by the National Socialists, and of the millions on millions of all confessions and all nations, victims of the
same hatred of the other man, the same anti-Semitism."[1] By reason
of this memory, Heidegger's analysis of Being-toward-death, on the
very point that seems most incontrovertible, remains, for Levinas,

unacceptable. Few passages of Levinas's relentless engagement with *Being and Time* summon and demand of him a more frequent and critical reading than the paragraphs that develop this analysis. He probes it again and again, in interminable dissections, as if the meditation on death that unfolds in these paragraphs were a frontal attack on the ethical, political, and above all philosophical challenge raised by the memory of the dead. That engagement undergirds the general architecture of Levinas's lectures at the Collège Philosophique in 1946–47, published as *Time and the Other*. It reemerges in *Totality and Infinity* (1961) at the core of the chapter devoted to "time and the ethical relation." It recurs a third time in one of Levinas's last lectures at the Sorbonne (1975–76), pronounced following the publication of *Otherwise Than Being; or, Beyond Essence*. These lectures, published under the title *Death and Time,* continue to wrestle with the existential analytic, just as, beyond the seven sessions devoted explicitly to Heidegger's thought, do all of Levinas's reflections on death, from his early writings to his last. Finally, when a colloquium is organized at the Collège International de la Philosophie in 1987 to mark the centennial of Heidegger's birth, it is significant that Levinas chooses to say, ultimately and briefly, what he finds fundamentally "important"[2] for him in *Being and Time* regarding the question of "dying for."[3]

Levinas's critique, however, varies from text to text. Each critical engagement is articulated in a unique way by some phenomenon whose consideration reveals something *missing* in Heidegger's analysis, the examination of which reveals the ponderous absence that is caused by reducing the analysis of our relation to death to our unshareable and non-substitutable anxiety before nothingness. In *Time and the Other,* it is the relation between solitude, suffering, and death; in *Totality and Infinity* it is the phenomenon of violence and murder; in "dying for" it is that of sacrifice. In each case, Levinas underscores the problematic nature of the same key points of Heidegger's analysis, of which four can be distinguished. The first concerns the way in which Heidegger makes of death *my* ownmost *possibility*. It bears on both the determination of death as "possibility"—that is as "ability" [*pouvoir*]—and on the appropriation that is the object of this possibility (on death as *mine*). The second point concerns the exclusive privilege that the author of *Being and Time* accords to anxiety to the detriment of any other emotion, notably fear. He does so by treating anxiety as the fundamental affect [*affection*] through which one decides one's relation to death as possibility, whether as something to flee or to assume. The third relates to Heidegger's exhortation to an authentic Being-toward-death and what he presumes to be "heroism," understood by Levinas as "a supreme lucidity and hence a supreme virility."[4] The last point, on which Levinas concentrates the most essential of his criticisms, follows from the first three. It addresses the fact that both the determination of anxiety as fundamental affect and the heroism of an authentic Being-toward-death imply one's abstraction from any relation toward others. Both assume *Dasein*'s solipsistic withdrawal into its relation to death. Neither the emotion provoked by the death of others (particularly the death, following *Being and Time*'s publication, of the victims of war and especially those of the Shoah, about which Heidegger, following the end of the war, had essentially nothing to say) nor the threat that the other's potential hostility (e.g., that of the executioner, or the hostility that is my own) suspends over our lives (as the possibility of murder), should or even could have a place within the limits of the analytic and be allowed to shed light on the relation to death. This is the consequence of *Dasein*'s confinement to solitude [*esseulement*] in the face of death. This is also the conclusion that Levinas could never accept in his own thought of death, exposed (or dedicated) as it was, as the thought of a survivor, to the memory of the victims of war: "In this way, *Dasein* would be proper, or properly thought—the care for being that, in its being for which it feels care, is destined for death. Consequently, it is at once anxious for being and before being [*pour l'être et devant l'être*] (that nothingness

that causes fear is also the nothingness that one wants). . . . Thus the
totality of the human being and of its own being-there is sought without any intervention by another, solely in *Dasein* as being-in-the-world.
The meaning of death is from the beginning interpreted as the *end* of
being-in-the-world, as annihilation."[5]

With reference to these four points, though reversing their order,
we can outline the principal features of Levinas's own analysis of the
relation to death. Although the object of this analysis is, in short,
to associate this relation with the transcendence of the other, it will
assume, like so many of the objections levied against Heidegger's text,
first, that death should not be understood as a possibility—the possibility of nothingness—but as that whose approach (imminence)
renders the subject completely powerless (and thus denies him the possibility of appropriation); second, that nothingness should not be sin-
gled out as the only thing about death that is feared (as the anxiety that
radically confines us to solitude)[6] but should be acknowledged [*donné
droit*] for another kind (or for several kinds) of affect [*affection*] and
emotion; and third and finally, that the responsibility that is engaged
in the relation to death should not be conceptualized as the "virility"
and "lucidity" of a solitary hero, but as responsibility for the other.

We should note that Levinas's objections are developed not only
through his engagement with Heidegger's text, but simultaneously
with that text's immediate posterity. Written in 1946–47, *Time and
the Other* reverberates with the echo of a book already discussed here,
Sartre's *Being and Nothingness,* whose impact on Levinas's audience
at the Collège Philosophique was, at the time, at least as considerable
as that of *Being and Time.* As shown in the previous chapter, this book
also grappled with the existential analytic of Being-toward-death.
This is not to say that Levinas read Heidegger through the prism of
Sartre's analysis. In fact, this is certainly not the case. But the objections he formulates nevertheless do bear the imprint of this other
book. His analyses intersect with those of Sartre (particularly when

they address the impossibility of thinking of [*my*] death as *my* possibility) as much as they take issue with them by freeing the thought of death from all thought of being and nothingness.

If this intersection with Sartre's thought is possible it is because Levinas's analysis of the relation to death is not an end in itself, but is inscribed strategically in a much broader project, one that informs all of Levinas's work, which is to contest the primacy of ontology—that is to say thought on being and nothingness—as set in motion by both Heidegger's and Sartre's work. The originality of Levinas's approach, therefore, is first of all its method. The objections he raises with regard to the existential analytic of Being-toward-death, as stated above, are not presented as frontal assaults, but emerge from the examination of phenomena that the existential analytic ignores: the relation between suffering and death (the imminence of death in suffering), the possibility of murder (*my* death as desired by the other), and sacrifice (my decision to die *in the place* of the other). Through the analysis of such phenomena, which resist ontological formulation, Levinas does not merely displace the existential analytic, but challenges it indirectly but more radically at its most fundamental level—that is, at the level at which it accords primacy to ontology in all thought about the relation to death and, indeed, to ontology *in general*. With the help of such phenomena, Levinas locates a place from which to think about death that is different from the one that traps thought in nothingness. It wrests the relation to death from the grip of Being (and from concern about the perseverance of Being) and from the anxiety of nothingness. Levinas writes in *Time and the Other,* as he articulates the analyses that he is proposing to undertake regarding death and suffering, "I even wonder how the principal trait of our relationship with death could have escaped philosophers' attention. It is not with the nothingness of death, of which we precisely know nothing, that the analysis must begin, but with the situation where something absolutely unknowable appears. Absolutely unknowable means foreign to all light, rendering every assumption of possibility impossible, but where we ourselves are seized."[7]

The death that approaches in a paroxysm of suffering . . . This is the theme with which Levinas sets in motion his refutation of the idea that Being-toward-death culminates in anxiety before nothingness. That refutation begins by pointing to a problem in *Being and Time* that arises from the existential analytic of Being-toward-death. By postulating that death is *Dasein*'s ownmost possibility, Heidegger's analysis abstains in effect from any consideration of death's approach. It does not differentiate between the relations toward death that one might entertain at different stages of one's life. It therefore ignores what death's imminence might signify regarding the relation to death for the person whom old age, illness, or some other condemnation has brought ineluctably closer to the final end. Heidegger does not want to deal with agony.

Antithetically to such ignorance—which is perhaps only the reverse side of a "heroic virility of an authentic Being-toward-death"—Levinas's *Time and the Other* begins with suffering, and examines death's approach closely. That is to say, it initiates the analysis of our relation to death at the moment when, exhausted, disarmed, and powerless, we find ourselves brutally dispossessed of all possibility, of all projection, which is to say, of all power. Levinas calls to mind how suffering exposes us to the "irredeemability of Being." To suffer means to find oneself in the absolute incapacity of escaping from Being, and therefore of experiencing [*éprouver*] nothingness. Suffering, for this reason, also constitutes the paroxysm of solitude. The subject, whose suffering invades his every thought, finds himself chained to the materiality of his body, which robs him of even that enjoyment of earthly nourishment that Levinas calls "hypostasis"—"the event by which the existent contracts its existing."[8]

Reading Levinas brings to mind Tolstoy's *The Death of Ivan Ilyich,* with its inimitable and meticulous description of this irredeemability of being in suffering. The Russian novelist analyzes with great precision how physical pain causes the protagonist, Ivan Ilyich, to lose all taste for the pleasures of life (meals, card games with friends, conversation) as well as all interest in activities that once enabled him to escape from his preoccupations [*se désenchaîner de lui-même*]. He loses, in other words, all orientation and any location [*repères*] in life beyond the parameters of his own pain. Words cannot break through his solitude—they cannot relieve or lighten "the burden the Self imposes on the I [*l'encombrement du moi par le soi*]," which Levinas sees as the culmination of physical suffering:

> The pain in his side went on wearing him down and seemed to be getting worse, nagging incessantly, while the taste in his mouth got more and more peculiar and he began to think that his breath smelt awful, and his appetite and strength fell away. The time for fooling himself was over: something new and dreadful was going on inside Ivan Ilyich, something significant, more significant than anything in his whole life. And he was the only one who knew it; the people around him didn't know, or didn't want to now—they thought that everything in the world was going on as before.[9]

But it is when Levinas and Tolstoy evoke the articulation between suffering and death that their analyses exhibit a most enlightening similarity. In *Time and the Other,* the analysis of suffering assumes meaning only when oriented toward that point—the point at which it is impossible to flee or to back out—at which the relationship with suffering opens up on the unknowable that is death—that is, on the experience of radical *alterity*. When suffering turns the subject inward into himself, the premonition of death in which suffering culminates places the subject "in relationship with what does not come from himself."[10] The exposure to suffering is inseparable from the need to know. The subject wants to know why he suffers and what can be done about it; he multiplies his consultations, with no satisfaction other than a short-lived hope. He relates everything to the evil that binds him, and does not tolerate anything, cannot relate to anything, that remains foreign to that evil. But as death approaches, it presses itself on the subject as that which he cannot appropriate—and about which or against which there is nothing he can do. Death articulates the mystery of an inappropriable unknown through the impossibility of nothingness, as signified by the irremissibility of suffering. Tolstoy's narrative reproduces the stages evoked by *Time and the Other* step by step. As the title suggests, it is also oriented toward this unknown that, according to Levinas, "is impossible to translate into terms of light—that is refractory to the intimacy of the self with the ego to which all our experiences return."[11] As death becomes imminent, the inward turn [*le retour sur soi*], the withdrawal into one's history, one's biography, the attachment to the film of one's life that locks the dying person into his own solitude, yields to the apprehension of an unknown over which the subject no longer has any power—and which by this very fact remains impervious to all forms of identification. For Ivan Ilyich, the terror of death is not anxiety about nothingness (the possibility of the impossibility of being), but apprehension regarding an unknown state, which cannot be reconciled with the rest of existence, an inappropriable mystery the fear of which eludes the binary, being and nothingness—a mystery that pertains neither to being nor to its impossibility: "With every minute that passed he sensed that, despite all his fighting and struggling, he was getting nearer and nearer to the thing that terrified him. He sensed that the pain came from being thrust into that black hole and, what was worse, not being able to get through. What was preventing him from getting through was his insistence that his life had been a good one. This vindication of his lifestyle was holding him down, preventing him from moving on, and causing him the greatest suffering."[12]

If we recall the three potential objections to Heidegger's analysis of Being-toward-death discussed above (and foregrounded in Levinas's reflections on death), we note that at least two of them are implicated in the effort to examine, together, solitude, suffering, agony, and death.[13] The first of these objections is that we can no longer consider death as *my* possibility or as *my* project when we focus on the last moments of life (marked by absolute powerlessness, of that extreme defenselessness that Levinas compares with the weeping of childhood). In these last moments, I do not relate to my death as to my ownmost possibility, but to this unknown that is characterized, once again, by its *radical alterity*. Death remains, until the very end, that which is impossible for me to make *my own*. Hence—and this is the second objection—death does not summon me to assume death heroically. Indeed, death invests the subject with a passiveness that signifies, for the subject, the end of all possible mastery ("the end of the subject's virility and heroism")[14]—and thus turns the project of an authentic Being-toward-death into a denial of death's mystery and a denial of its very alterity:

> My mastery, my virility, my heroism as a subject can be neither virility nor heroism in relation to death. There is in the suffering at the heart of which we have grasped this nearness of death—and still at the level of the phenomenon—this reversal of the subject's activity into passivity. This is not just in the instant of suffering where, backed against being, I still grasp it and am still the subject of suffering, but in the crying and sobbing toward which suffering is inverted. Where suffering attains its purity, where there is no longer anything between us and it, the supreme responsibility, of this extreme assumption turns into supreme irresponsibility, into infancy.[15]

But making suffering—or rather its inversion, in *weeping* and *sob-bing*—the point of departure for thinking about death has yet another consequence. Because it replaces heroism with the passiveness of the subject, it opens up another problematic, though one that *Time and the Other* does not thematize explicitly, which is the responsibility for the care and aid that the dying person enjoins. More generally, it enables the analysis, which *Being and Time* ignores, of the subject's responsibility when confronted by the death of others. What is the nature [*ordre*] of this responsibility? How does the transcendence of the other intervene in our relation to this radical alterity that is death, the unknown? Levinas takes these questions up in *Totality and Infinity,* where he reprises the question of death, but with new ramifications. He will also explore them in his lectures on *Death and Time,* and in his address titled "Dying For." Unlike *Time and the Other,* these works summon new points of departure—murder and sacrifice—that represent jointly a more direct challenge to *Dasein*'s confinement to solitude in its relation to death.

Totality and Infinity, like *Time and the Other,* begins its reflections on death by refusing to inscribe them in the binary, being and nothing-ness. But the phenomenon toward which Levinas directs his atten-tion in order to ground his refutation does not concern the subject alone—that is, the subject as enclosed in the solitude of his hyposta-sis. Recalling that "death is interpreted in the whole philosophical and religious tradition either as a passage to nothingness or as a passage to another existence, continuing in a new setting," it is the analysis of the moral impossibility of annihilating the other, as expressed by the face of the other, that will enable Levinas to challenge "the truth of the thought that situates death either in nothingness or in being."[16] If it is true that Levinas's reflections on death are inseparable from the memory of the crimes of the twentieth century—which is one of the reasons why his reflections are directed against thought on being and death—his choice of murder as the point at which to *begin to speak of death* inscribes (even more than *Time and the Other*) his opposition to Heidegger's thought (and no doubt to Sartre's thought as well) in the memory of the violence that humankind inflicts on itself. "Inscribes," that is, at least implicitly—as if better to express the impossibility of thinking about death without being immediately challenged and perturbed by *that will to annihilation* [*volonté d'anéantissement*] that condemned millions upon millions of human beings to extermination.

But in this case it is not annihilation, but the will, that constitutes the obligatory point of departure. This is the choice that Levinas makes in *Totality and Infinity*—a choice that will considerably help reinforce the three objections presented above. In effect, as point of departure it introduces a twofold problematic into the thought of death. The first, which encapsulates Levinas' entire trajectory in addressing the question of murder, is that of murder's prohibition, as expressed in the face of the other. That prohibition is itself only meaningful to the extent that murder is a possibility—a possibility that is always primary [*première*]. In the complex architecture of *Being and Time,* Heidegger never asks *from what direction* death might come—and it is for this reason that he overlooks the profusion of crimes, the acts of political violence, the misery, the famine, the executions and exterminations, that form the fabric of history. According to *Being and Time, Dasein* relates to the possibility of its own death, independently of the will of others who can "will my death," transgress the prohibition of murder, and of the forces that can organize, instrumentalize, or embody this will. *Totality and Infinity* gives license to such threats, and thus reinscribes the relation to death within the sphere of interpersonal relations. In doing so it also suggests that this relation depends primarily on ethics and politics—and not on ontology. Everything is thus displaced.

The point of departure for thinking about death should not be one's anxiety in the face of nothingness, but the "fear that I can have for my being"—of this primary fear that stems less from the knowledge of death than from the apprehension of all that makes death possible, of all that renders its approach more menacing for my being. Relating to my own death, I think, first, of all the things that might happen that could threaten my life, the violence that is always possible and that could place my being in peril—the violence that is bounded by no horizon since its irruption is always unforeseeable: "It is not the knowledge of death that defines menace; it is in the imminence of death, in its irreducible oncoming movement, that menace originally consists, that the 'knowledge of death' is (if one may put it so) uttered and articulated. Fear measures this movement."[17]

It is this violence, which Heidegger never mentions, that assigns to the other its fundamental place in our relation to death. For this violence is, first of all, that of history. To read Levinas is to think about the millions of human beings exposed to imminent arrest and execution, to deportation and extermination, the victims of war, of inhumane labor, of misery and famine, for whom, over the centuries, the relation to death assumed no other form than this "coming ever closer" [*mouvement d'approche*]—than this exposure to the homicidal will of the other. More generally, there are all those plausible causes of my death that seem more or less clearly to reflect possible ill will. Whatever these other causes might be (accidents, illness, etc.) they are forever inseparable from the hypothesis of what Levinas calls "malevolence" [*malveillance*]—even if supernatural. Death is never *mine*, because I associate it with external causes that escape my power and knowledge—causes whose alterity is irreducible. Heidegger's thematization of *Dasein*'s solitude in the face of death is thus shattered, in a first sense, by the hypothesis of this ill will (human or divine) that makes of the other, as of the world more generally, a hostile being. No one faces death alone because no one can imagine that one might be *solely* responsible for it. To what or to whom we might assign this responsibility does not matter. No one can imagine that we must assume the possibility of death, *heroically,* without dread of all the forces, all the *other* occasions, inappropriable in their essence, that might place us in peril:

> The Other, inseparable from the very event of transcendence, is situated in the region from which death, possibly murder, comes. The unwonted hour of its coming approaches as the hour of fate fixed by someone. Hostile and malevolent powers, more wily, more clever than I, absolutely other and only thereby hostile, retain its secret. Death, in its absurdity, maintains an interpersonal order, in which it tends to take on a signification. . . . The things that bring death to me, being graspable and subject to labor, obstacles rather than menaces, refer to a malevolence, are the residue of a bad will which surprises and stalks.[18]

The other therefore belongs to that region that death comes from. And yet, what I read in the face of the other is entirely different [*tout autre*]: the prohibition of murder, the impossibility by right of annihilating him [*l'impossibilité de droit de son anéantissement*]—in which, at each encounter, his transcendence expresses itself. It is here that we find the force, the singularity of Levinas's method. If the place of the other were limited to the possibility of murder, if this were the final word in our relation to death, then there would be no solution other than war. But because this possibility is bracketed, neglected, or ignored, because the thought of death, confined by the binary being and nothingness, provides no license for fear, there is no acknowledgment of either the necessity of ethics (beyond ontology) or of politics (articulated by some ethics). For Levinas, this in the end was without doubt the unacceptable limitation of Heidegger's analyses of Being-toward-death. And perhaps this is also why, in the end, it was the important question that *Being and Time,* for him, was raising. Having failed to take into account the degree to which perseverance in Being is bound up with the possibility of murder, and having thereby failed to think through what, in our relation conjointly to the other and to death, might open up other possibilities (those in which ethics and politics are grounded), Heidegger's analysis boils down *to the same thing* as thought of war—thought that makes war the last word in the relation of beings to one another, without concern for its victims.

In our relation to death, the place of the other is located in the possibilities both of murder and its prohibition. The two go together. But because these possibilities are complementary and because their complementarity suspends or *postpones* war, they designate a third location whose disclosure brings to completion Levinas's interrogation of *Dasein*'s solitude. This third location takes us back to the articulation between suffering and death, the articulation that is found in the expectation, in the *hope* that the other will bring me care, relief, and help: "The solitude of death does not make the Other vanish, but remains in a consciousness of hostility, and consequently still renders possible an appeal to the Other, to his friendship and his medication. The doctor is an *a priori* principle of human mortality. Death approaches in the fear of someone, and hopes in someone. 'The Eternal brings death and brings life.' A social conjuncture is maintained in this menace. It does not sink into the anxiety that would transform it into a menace."[19]

No one refers to the possibility of his or her own death without expecting and hoping for some assistance from the other—that is, for some postponement of the final reckoning. But if it is true that "murder, rather than being one of the occasions of dying, [is] inseparable from death,"[20] and if it is therefore true that the approach of death (in the form of murder) belongs constitutively to the relation to the other, then this *postponement* of death, far from being a mere question of medication, also gestures more generally to the time of the political [*au temps de la politique*]. Our relation to death is not separable from our need for protection *against death*—that is, against all the threats that make the possibility of death more or less probable, imminent, or urgent. This Being-against-death, always shared, defines and differentiates between "social conditions" [*conjonctures*]. It is because such conditions are not always and everywhere the same that our relation to death is not universalizable. In the face of such threats— which include a number of forms of violent death: war, terrorism, genocide, homicidal repression, famine, misery, lack of access to medical care, and all the forms that contempt for life can generate in great variety—we are not equal. Thus, in our effort to understand the essence of our relation to death, setting out from murder provides us additionally with the means to differentiate (and perhaps to judge) such "social conditions," and, with them, the institutions through which decisions are made regarding the nature and the extent of the *postponement*. Absent such a starting place, thought of death ignores such distinctions, ignores the consideration or appreciation of the variety forms that violence can assume. While it holds fear (one's own, and that of others) in heroic contempt, it ignores politics, just as it ignores the alienation of the will by the other:

> The violence of death threatens as a tyranny, as though proceeding from a foreign will. The order of necessity that is carried out in death is not like an implacable law of determinism governing a totality but is rather like the alienation of my will by the Other. . . . But if the will is mortal and susceptible to violence from a blade of steel, from the chemistry of poison, from hunger and thirst, if it is a body maintaining itself between health and sickness, this is not only because it would be surrounded by nothingness. This nothingness is an interval beyond which lurks a hostile will. I am a passivity threatened not only by nothingness in my being, but by a will in my will.[21]

Protecting oneself from violence is thus the first possibility provided by the postponement of death. Being-against-death is situated in the temporal interval that separates me from this radical unknown, which *Totality and Infinity*, reprising the terminology of *Time and the Other*, amplifies by using the term "mystery." "Amplifies" because, if the mysterious character of death is forever bound to my powerlessness over it, it becomes affixed to its unpredictability—unpredictability not of the threat itself, but of the execution of that threat. The "mystery" of death, in which my fear takes root, is, therefore, also the mystery of violence. In the end, one knows neither when, nor from what direction it might come.

But is protection the last word for "postponement"? Is it the only way that postponement enables us to "vanquish" death, however provisionally? If this were the case, one could hardly understand protection's affinity with the transcendence of the other—that is, with the prohibition of murder that is expressed in the face of the other. Protection is assured only by the creation of institutions, which, Levinas reminds us, secure nothing more (though nothing less) than "a meaningful, *but impersonal* world."[22] It does not necessarily bring us back to egoism, but neither does it bear witness to this "desire for the Other" that constitutes the only way to respond to the other's *transcendence*. Our relation to death is absolutely inseparable from this desire. It is inseparable from this desire because *postponement*, per se, brings us back necessarily to the questions: "How can we overcome death?" "Can we in fact overcome death?" "Is protecting oneself from death a victory?"[23] Levinas's work, in its entirety, may perhaps have had no other objective than to find answers to these questions. It seeks the answers by placing the time that separates us from death under the sign of desire for the other—under the sign of responsibility for the other— by showing, in book after book, that *only* this exposure to the other can endow this time with meaning: "The will, already betrayal and alienation of itself but postponing this betrayal, on the way to death but a death ever future, exposed to death but not *immediately,* has time to be for the Other, and thus to recover meaning despite death. This existence for the Other, this Desire of the other, this goodness liberated from the egoist gravitation, nonetheless retains a personal character. . . . The Desire into which the threatened will dissolves no longer defends the powers of a will, but, as the goodness whose meaning death cannot efface, has its center outside of itself."[24]

Responsibility for the other upends our relation to death completely and utterly, just as it upends the meaning of fear. Fear can no longer be detached from the way in which I am affected by the death *of the other,* and, even before the trial of this death, from the way in which I anticipate and envision with apprehension [*appréhende*] the passing of the other. Although *Totality and Infinity* stops at the threshold of this upending, it will form the core of Levinas's reflection on death in most of the work that will follow. In his 1975–76 lectures, *God, Death, and Time,* his reflection is articulated by the concern to conceptualize the relation to death *otherwise* than by referring it to "the threat that weighs upon my being."[25] In the *postponement,* it is the relation to the other *and to his death* that alone is capable of breaking down my identity as ego [*moi*]. It is this relation that is able to rupture the identity of the self [*même*] in the ego. How does this relation come about? What forms does it assume? Of these we shall examine two. The first is the form that turns this responsibility into the responsibility of the survivor. If it is true that the face of the other expresses his transcendence, that it addresses signs to me to which I must respond, then it is this expression and this address that the death of the other takes away. Well do we know, as we are confronted for the last time by the dormant face of the deceased, how much we try to attribute a smile to him, some form of expressivity, to remember him by seeking out, in his immobility, the last sign he addressed to us. But we also know that his face has always been the very expression of his mortality, that his transcendence is not separable from his vulnerability. It is this extreme fragility that will have always enjoined our responsibility: "But in its expression, in its mortality, the face before me summons me, calls for me, begs for me, as if the invisible death that must be faced by the Other, pure otherness, separated, in some way, from any whole, were my business. It is as if that invisible death, ignored by the Other, whom already it concerns by the nakedness of its face, were already 'regarding' me prior to confronting me, and becoming the death that stares me in the face."[26]

This is the high point of Levinas' confrontation with Heidegger's analysis of Being-toward-death. Although it is true that Heidegger's analysis seeks to summon each of us to assume our own mortality— to the extent that this mortality is our own, and cannot be *replaced* or *shared*—it excludes in principle, if not my ability to be the guardian of another life, at least my ability to place before the consideration of *my* own death this watchfulness or this vigilance, this attention or this basic availability. For Levinas, on the contrary, the death of the other comes *before* my own. I am *first and foremost* responsible for the death of the other. I am always under suspicion for not having taken adequate care of him whose face implored my responsibility, for having been indifferent to his suffering, inattentive to the perils that surrounded him, in a word, for having abandoned him to his "mortal solitude."[27] In the *postponement* that separates me from my own death, this responsibility alone, which precedes in me any concern for perseverance in Being, gives meaning to time. It alone separates me from myself. Whether expounded in his present lecture or in his discourse on the face, it is a responsibility that Levinas insists, in "Dying for . . . ," "cannot, *after the trials of the twentieth century,* be construed as signifying the trite platitudes of a verbose idealism."[28]

This is why ethics precedes politics. This is why the exposure to the infinite responsibility that is summoned by the vulnerability of the other (of any other, and not simply my fellow citizen, my fellow countryman, my brother, etc.) comes before *my* protection, even if the latter were to extend, in a manner that is always selective and limited, to others other than myself. And this is why what seemed unthinkable in the general economy of *Being and Time*—*to die for the other* (in the place of the other)—becomes the culminating point, the ultimate and elliptical point of Levinas's thought on death. It is significant that the last word in his thought is about sacrifice—the sacrifice that becomes the obverse of the image of the care [*souci*] to persevere in Being, and, simultaneously, of that heroic virility and lucidity of the subject that Levinas repudiated in *Time and the Other*: "Sacrifice cannot find a place for itself in an order divided between the authentic and the unauthentic. Does not the relationship to the other in sacrifice, in which the death of the other preoccupies the human *being-there* [*Dasein*] before his own death, indicate precisely a beyond ontology—or a before ontology—while at the same time also determining—or revealing—a responsibility for the other, and through that responsibility a human 'I' that is neither the substantial identity of a subject nor the *Eigentlichkeit* in the 'mineness' of being?"[29]

As paradoxical as it might seem, it is a "victory over death"—a victory over the attachment to Being and over the anxious apprehension before nothingness.[30] It is also a victory over the paralysis of fear in the face of perils that herald the approach of death. If the wars of the twentieth century signify the exponential multiplication of such perils, if history continues to invent new kinds of similar perils, both war and history have also offered examples of just such a victory in the template of "the just"—of those who risked their lives and who so often gave up their lives for another. Perhaps Levinas sought to bring them back to mind by asking, one last time, the question of what is missing in *Being and Time*.

4

Unrelenting War

⤜ Jan Patočka ⤛

> The first world war is the decisive event in the history of the twentieth century. It determined its entire character. It was this war that demonstrated that the *transformation* of the world into a laboratory for releasing reserves of energy accumulated over billions of years can be achieved only by means of wars.
>
> —JAN PATOČKA, *Heretical Essays in the Philosophy of History*

What should we remember of the wars of the twentieth century? How can the memory of the millions upon millions of lives sacrificed on all fronts, of the countless victims of organized famine, forced labor, deportation, and the extermination camps be inscribed in our thought? And what form should that memory assume? What is thought's responsibility in opening itself to that memory? In all probability no great philosophy of the second half of the twentieth century has evaded these questions, no matter how implicitly or allusively they may have been treated. Such questions could not fail to have an impact on ethics, political thought, law, history, and even thought on science and technology. We saw how true this was of Levinas's work, in which the primacy of ethics (the exposure to the irreducible alterity of the other) over ontology (reflection on being and nothingness) is inseparable from the memory of war. It is equally true of Patočka, whose *Heretical Essays* culminate in reflections of a rare dramatic intensity on "the wars of the twentieth century."

Patočka's thought, however, is not merely or even principally the product of remembrance. Responsibility for Patočka is inscribed in neither obligation nor in mourning, but rather—in succession—in the descriptive analysis of the patterns underlying these wars (what they teach us about the world), in the declaration of the convulsions that the wars *should have* produced (our relation to the world), and finally in the examination of the reasons why they utterly failed to produce them. Patočka's work presents itself, therefore, both as a meditation on war and as a critique of the illusion of peace. It measures the extent to which, despite the sacrifice of millions of victims (and perhaps even *because* of it), war *continues* [*continue*] in peace. The world remains *the same,* and our existence remains subject to the same imperatives as those that produced war, to what Patočka calls the "forces of the day." What are these forces? How are they able to bind existence as if in chains, and in so doing confiscate the memory of war? Why is it that every peace seems ineluctably to lay the ground for new wars to come? The originality of Patočka's approach is in showing how war is inseparable from our relation to death. The "forces of death" bind *us* through our fear of death. The thread that unifies this chapter is thus to understand, in the light of *Heretical Essays,* the articulation between the meaning of the world, as revealed by war, and the thought of death as organized by war. We will also try to grasp how an alternative meaning of both the world and death might emerge from the experience of the front, understood as sacrifice (whose generalizability we must try to determine).

What then do the wars of the twentieth century teach us about the world? This is the question that Patočka seeks to answer in the first pages of the essay devoted to them by proposing, as did Rosenzweig sixty years earlier, an interpretation of the motivations that led to the First World War.[1] But whereas the author of *The Star of Redemption* understood the war as the result of the mortal combat that the peoples of Europe inflicted on themselves with a view to their election (which presupposed the appropriation of the world), the author of *Heretical Essays* maintains that the war revealed how much the world finds its meaning through an apportionment [*partage*] of force and power [*puissance*]:[2] "The shared idea in the background of the first world war was the slowly germinating conviction that there is nothing such as a factual, objective meaning of the world and of things, and that it is up to strength and power to create such meaning within the realm accessible to humans."[3]

Patočka's portrayal of the belligerents highlights their relation to this apportionment as it stood on the eve of war. Whereas the allies (essentially France and Great Britain) were attached to a global status quo that had long favored them, Germany stood out by its desire to change that status quo in pursuit of new principles that it had defended in Europe, and which justified, in its estimation, its claim to a position of preponderance. These new principles emerged from "the ever deepening techno-scientific aspect of [German] life," whereby German society "vehemently and ruthlessly pursued the accumulation of building, organizing, transforming energy."[4] It was the will to maintain the status quo, or alternatively the decision to reject it, that dictated the alliances. At stake was the power to transform Europe into a formidable energetic complex, and the exploitation and liberation of the world's energy reserves. The war was the manifestation, or the blunt translation, of what Patočka, reading Husserl and Heidegger, describes (in other work that is contemporary with *Heretical Essays*) as a new world age, a new era—the technical era—that had dawned on the world: "Because the technical age is one of calculable resources and their use which can be 'on order,' and because that age seeks to isolate and squeeze out of everything and everyone the utmost possible performance, it is also an age of unaccustomed unfolding of power. The most powerful means of its escalation, however, proved to be contradiction, dissension and conflict. In conflict it becomes especially clear that man as such is not understood as dominant but is included as something that is 'on order.'"[5]

It is not difficult to discern in this evocation of the technical, as the disposing [*mise à disposition*] and the setting-upon [*rentabilisa-tion*] of quantifiable resources, the very terms of Heidegger's analysis of technology [*technique*] (as *Gestell*), to which Patočka will return again and again in the 1970s. Beyond its heritage and historical con-text, the reading that Patočka proposes, and the application of Hei-degger's terms to make sense of the wars of the twentieth century, enable the author of *Heretical Essays* to discern two outcomes that will lend considerable importance to his analysis. First, by relating the wars to the apportionment of force and power (conceptualized as the exploitation and liberation of the world's energy reserves), he ex-plains why, in times of peace and in defiance of all the institutions that strive to prevent war, of all the rules of law, and of all the agree-ments and treaties, *war continues*. The "forces of the day" that ordain and organize the peace are the same forces as those that propelled millions upon millions of human beings into the torment of war. They forever prepare humanity for new wars because, whatever one might think about the apportionment of forces and the occasional guaran-tees that accompany it, nothing is ever definitive and nothing is ever acceptable to everyone. If the great "lesson" of the First World War was to show that while the world found its meaning in the struggle for force and power, peace (which, it would seem, brought an end to war) opened no perspective on an *alternative* meaning. As Patočka reviews the balance of forces during the interwar period, prior to the outbreak of World War Two, and during the Cold War, he can only confirm this observation. There is no doubt that in our day the wars of the Near and Middle East, the multiple threats linked to the appro-priation of oil reserves, and the availability of nuclear energy would confirm Patočka in his conviction that the imperatives of peace are *the same* as those that lead to war. On the one hand these imperatives are grounded in the fact that the defense of the status quo (concerning the apportionment of force and power) is unacceptable for some and of vital importance for others; and on the other hand they are grounded in the need for accumulated force to be discharged: "Why must the energetic transformation of the world take on the form of war? Because war, acute confrontation, is the most intensive means for the rapid release of accumulated forces. Conflict is the great instrument which, mythologically speaking, Force used in its transition from potency to actuality. In this process humans as well as individual peoples serve merely as tools."[6]

The second outcome of Patočka's analysis (an analysis that Heidegger, by the way, never attempted) is its ability to help us understand how the meaning of the world imposed by force and power is *doubly* linked to the relation to death. It is linked first by the high price—the millions of sacrificed lives—that the "forces of the day" exact to satisfy the requirements of their calculations. From this perspective, understanding the wars of the twentieth century in Patočka's terms means dropping the mask and measuring, with unnerving clarity, the significance of the war deaths for peace, when peace, from whatever angle we look at it, is itself nothing other than the *continuation of war*. What does it mean "to die for the fatherland," or "to die for freedom"? Although the questions provoked by these expressions have haunted philosophy and literature in the twentieth century, Patočka measures the extent to which they can be instrumentalized when appropriated by the peace for which the dead paid the price— when, in other words, the forces of the day *claim* them as they nevertheless prepare for other wars. Reflecting on the wars of the twentieth century and their countless victims, both civilian and military, one is forced to return to the unfathomable, sometimes scandalous, and always disturbing question, "What for?" [*Pour quoi?*]. The question has not been put to rest in the decades that separate us from the Second World War and from Patočka's death. On the contrary, each new conflict, each new sacrifice of whole generations, on all fronts, bearing the proper names of places (Vietnam, Korea, Afghanistan, and so many others), raises the question anew. The power of the last chapter of *Heretical Essays* will always be felt because of its willingness—once the celebrations, the commemorations, the customary tributes, the official histories and speeches are over and done—to risk the question of the why and wherefore of this cult of "those who died for the fatherland," "those who died on the field of honor" "those who died for . . . ," a cult that, in times of peace, tames and hijacks war's horrors and the irreducible and absolute character of the experience of the front (in the broadest understanding of that term). What is always being camouflaged is nothing other than the ends, the objectives, the interests, the apportionment of force and power for which these lives were sacrificed: "Peace and the day necessarily rule by sending humans to death in order to assure *others* a day in the future in the form of progress, of a free and increasing expansion, of possibilities they lack today. Of those whom it sacrifices it demands, by contrast, *endurance* in the face of death. That indicates a dark awareness that life is not everything, that it can sacrifice itself. That self-sacrifice, that surrender, is what is called for."[7]

But this appropriation of the victims of war, this confiscation of their sacrifice, is merely one of two aspects of the relation to death that are brought to light by an interpretation that places the wars of the twentieth century—the world wars, or the world at war—under the sign of a death struggle for the (technical and energetic) disposing [*disposition*] of force and power. Because "war continues" in peacetime, and because the forces of the day are always preparing the ground for more sacrifices—including the sacrifice of entire generations to whom they had promised life and durable peace (as is always the case in the aftermath of war)—and because no promise of peace can resist the imperative of force and power that gives the world meaning, humanity lives forever under the *threat* of violent death. War casts this *threat* as a shadow over the lives of every one of us. It binds the memory of war (and its continuation) to life (which means a certain relation to death) in ways that Patočka is at pains to decipher. For one must separate the significance of this threat into two components. On the one hand, the "forces of the day" (the reign of peace, that is, of the peace that prepares the ground for war) attach each of us to a life (our life) that becomes for each of us the supreme value. The "forces of the day" multiply protections, guarantees, and assurances. They make of each singular existence a life that is protected from the thousand and one perils that might befall it. On the other hand, however (and because anything is possible in war), these same "forces of the day" (which are calculating their power and force) consider death of negligible importance. They are ready to renounce all the protections they provide and to expose each and every one of us (and in the most direct manner) to the peril of death if their computations demand it. What disappears in this case is the meaning of death itself. Death ceases to be meaningful. It becomes something of no consequence, given the imperatives revealed by the calculations of the forces of the day (as every war proves, every day, year after year, on every continent, as newspapers and television networks amass data on the number of war's victims): "For the forces of the day, conversely, death does not exist, they function as if there was no death, or, as noted, they plan death impersonally and statistically, as if it were merely a reassignment of roles. Thus in the will to war, day and life rule with the help of death. . . . Those who cannot break free of the rule of peace, of the day, of life in a mode that excludes death and closes its eyes before it, can never free themselves of war."[8]

The paradox of the "forces of the day" is that their apparent protection of life—their attachment to life—boils down to a failure to recognize the meaning of death. They use death; they turn it into an ever-available means with which to pursue their ends; and at the same time they inscribe it with an abstract, subsidiary, and accidental significance. The dead always end up being registered in some macabre catalog that presumes to be the last word regarding their sacrifice.

Such is the fundamental ambivalence of the relation to death (and thus to life) that emerges from a world that derives meaning from the sole apportionment of force and power—in contempt of every legislative structure and every international institution that exists. "Day, peace, and life"—to reprise Patočka's interrelated terms—tighten their grip on the body and soul of each individual by means of death. By making life the supreme value, the "forces of the day" turn death into the supreme threat. To satisfy the growing demands of the citizenry they promise to protect life, and they multiply the measures that seek to secure this end. Science and technology are themselves made to service this need for security. In his portrayal of the twentieth century, as in the portrayals of so many of those who came before and after him, the author of *Heretical Essays* underscores the extent to which the postwar decades, in Europe and in other parts of the developed world, went down this path. Whatever their degree of economic prosperity, however important their social achievements, the peoples of the developed world all moved in the direction of a reciprocal growth in their demand for protection and their feeling of security, which now applied to all spheres of life. There loomed everywhere the vital need to construct ramparts against death, so as no longer to have to think about it. Europe succeeded in this regard at the cost no doubt of what Patočka calls, without hesitation, its "demobilization," the illusion of a peace that has definitively removed the specter of war.

And yet *war continued*—and still continues—because this increased protection was and still is nothing more than the complement of the unequal apportionment of force and power. Misery, famine, the lack of access to the most elementary level of care, which prevail in much of the world, present the other side of this protection of the affluent. The relation to death (to all that threatens life) divides the world, just as does the apportionment of force and power: "The gigantic work of economic renewal, the unheard-of, even undreamed-of social achievement which blossomed in a Europe excluded from world history, shows that this continent has opted for demobilization because it has no other option. That contributes to the deepening of the gap between the *blessed haves* and those who are dying of hunger on a planet rich in energy—thus intensifying the *state of war*."[9]

The final chapter of *Heretical Essays,* in this regard, does not deviate from that apprehensiveness that characterizes Patočka's reflections on Europe, beginning with his introduction, also written in the 1970s, to *Plato and Europe.*[10] If the two world wars were first and foremost European wars (which drew the rest of the world in), if they trace their origins back to the apportionment of force and power in Europe, the continuation of these wars in the second half of the twentieth century and the first years of the twenty-first century is linked inseparably to the shift in this apportionment [*décentrage de ce partage*]. It now engages Europe's relation to its "alterities"—that is, the gap, which has become insupportable, between, on the one hand, those whom the apportionment favors, who cling *at any price* to the advantages and privileges (to the relation to death, everywhere secured and protected) that this apportionment enables, and, on the other, those whom this apportionment condemns to misery. There can be no doubt that if Patočka could see, on the one hand, how Europe protects itself from its "alterities," the ramparts it erects (e.g., against migration flows) so as to assure its security and protect its comfort, and, on the other hand, the increasingly desperate attempts to overcome these barriers, he would perceive better than anyone the veneer that "the continuation of war" has assumed in our day.[11]

The "forces of the day" benefit from the ambivalence in our relation to death. The fear of death (which shackles life) is the principal motif that plunges humanity into violence and war. It makes humanity available for the conflicts of the day and continually renews its

predisposition toward possible sacrifice. Proof of this predisposition
is the fact that, despite all the promises heard in the aftermath of war—
promises made in the name of future generations—no generation is
ever assured of not being sacrificed in some conflict to come. However great the commitment to peace, however important the degree
of "demobilization," the unequal apportionment [*partition*] of force
and power foments conditions such that the desire for peace, among
both those who have benefited from it and those who have been dis-
advantaged, capitulates one day to the will to war incited by the perils that inequality has wrought, whether real, fictitious, fantasized, or
instrumentally invented: "Peace, the day rely on death as the means
of maximal human unfreedom, as shackled humans refuse to see, but
which is present as *vis a tergo,* as the terror that drives humans even
into fire—death, chaining humans to life and rendering them most
manipulable."[12]

This is the cord that ties the meaning of a world to the relation to
death. It is a world destined to be dominated by technology and the
exploitation (unto exhaustion) of energy resources. The temptation
is great to surrender to nihilism, whose specter is certainly one that
haunts *Heretical Essays,* and one that the essays seek to confront. But
how does one escape the despair and discouragement that this *continuation* of war in peace ineluctably produces, and the fear and dis-
may that no institution, no system of protection can placate? The
final pages of Patočka's work grapple forcefully with these questions,
and engage with them from the most difficult and puzzling angle. If
it is true that the reduction of the world to an apportionment of force
and power dramatically culminates in the sacrifice of human lives as
the price for victory (as well as in other forms of contempt for life,
like the compromise with misery, with famine, with the refusal of assistance, and with all the terrors that this apportionment implies), then
our analysis must begin with this sacrifice. It must start here because
the deaths themselves cannot be reduced to the ciphers of some kind

of morbid balance sheet, even though the "forces of the day," imitated by the printed press and the television networks, attempt to do just that.

The death of the victims, of the millions upon millions of lives that are sacrificed, *transcends* passing calculations regarding life and peace. Patočka makes this claim with great force in a study of technology that he wrote at about the same time as *Heretical Essays,* a study that echoes with the remembrance of the tribute of war as well as of revolution (and thus required courage to write in the 1970s), neither of which escapes the fascination of such calculations: "The experience of a sacrifice . . . is now one of the most powerful experiences of our epoch, so powerful and definitive that humankind for the most part has not managed to come to terms with it and flees from it precisely into a technical understanding of being. . . . *Revolutionary and war-like conflicts* of our century were born of and borne by the spirit of a technical domination of the world; but those who had to bear the cost were in no case a mere store of disposable resources, but something quite irreducible to that. That precisely comes to the fore when we speak of sacrifices."[13]

One question remains. In what sense does the sacrifice of soldiers, on all fronts, as well as of the victims, both civilian and military, of all wars—including economic wars that are hardly less deadly than armed conflicts—*transcend* the apportionment of force and power? It is no accident that Patočka uses the word *transcendence* at precisely the point where attention is directed to the victims, as victims. Patočka's use of the word brings his thought in proximity to that of Levinas, for whom, as we saw, the question of sacrifice is a familiar one. Moreover, as we have observed, it becomes increasingly clear that the question of sacrifice, along with that of death (and heroism, and "dying for . . . ") is one of the axes around which philosophy in the last half of the twentieth century has tenaciously revolved. The organizing thread that guides the author of *Heretical Essays,* and which confers on his thinking its singularity, is provided by the experience of the front (notably that of the First World War) as narrated by a Teilhard de Chardin or an Ernst Jünger. Patočka focuses on the survivors [*revenants*]—on those who, having endured this "absolute experience," cannot assent to the relativity of the sacrifice, to the relativity of the renunciation of life that the "forces of everydayness" have exacted. Two meanings of sacrifice enter into opposition—and with them two relations to death, whose radical incompatibility must be exposed. The first involves thinking "about life and death," as characterized, at every stage, as we have seen, by its power of alienation and bondage. The victims of war, of all wars, are, according to this thinking, nothing more than the tribute offered up for all our attachments (for all that roots life in a complex system of fears and protections): "Peace transformed into a will to war could objectify and externalize humans as long as they were ruled by the day, by the hope of everydayness, of a profession, of a career, simply possibilities for which they must fear and which feel threatened."[14]

The second consists in turning the sacrifice inflicted upon millions and millions of human beings on all fronts back against the "forces of everydayness." This second understanding of sacrifice resists the power of alienation (which has its source in the instrumentalization of sacrifice) with a countervailing power to emancipate and destabilize. To discern in sacrifice its "absolute meaning," as Patočka tries to do, is not to "sacramentalize" it—and certainly not to promote or enjoin it—but to acknowledge that its significance, which cannot be reduced to some or other "calculation for peace," provokes unease by its very absoluteness, and indeed casts doubt on the authority and self-evidence of this same calculation. This acknowledgment comes from the refusal to see the victims, sacrificed on the altar of peace as interest, continue to serve this same interest unto death *and beyond*. Writing in the 1970s, the author of *Heretical Essays* was easily able to measure the extraordinary vacuity of oratory (of all oratory) that advanced one or the other of these claims in order to justify past fatalities and future sacrifices.

If the radical incompatibility of these two understandings of sacrifice is in fact meaningful, it is because of the abyss that separates the *unjustifiability* of death, as demanded and granted, from its *justifications*. Whether these latter go by the name of socialism, democratic freedom, progress, independence, or by the many other complements of "dying *for* . . ." or "dying *in the name of* . . ."—none holds up, *as justification*, if inscribed in the apportionment, forever bellicose, of force and power. No justification holds up if it subscribes, over and over again, to the multiple imperatives of a world divided, whose entire meaning is concentrated in this distinctive apportionment, which is to say in the figures, the statistics, the quantified studies that depict it, and in the reports, plans, and programs that exacerbate it:

> Now, however, comes the upheaval, shaking that peace and its planning, its programs and its ideas of progress *indifferent to mortality*. All everydayness, all visions of future life pale before the simple peak on which humans find themselves standing. In face of that, all the ideas of socialism, of progress, of democratic spontaneity, of independence and freedom appear impoverished, neither viable nor tangible. They achieve their full meaning not in themselves but only where they are derived from that peak and lead back to it in turn. Where they lead humans to bring about such a transformation of their whole lives, their entire existence.[15]

If we are to take up the question of the meaning of the world anew, we must therefore begin with our condition as "mortal beings." This is where we should have started long ago so as to destabilize the pretensions of the forces of the day and the imperious constraints of an everyday existence exposed to the fear of death. Patočka, developing

a cosmology that recalls the thought of Heraclitus, calls this destabi-
lization "the preponderance of the Night."[16] But what is the nature of
this preponderance? The response to this question must include three
elements. The first is the affirmation that death is not a trifle [*n'est
pas rien*], and that nothing can justify it. As long as peace, however
organized, is grounded in the denial [*déni*] of war, as long as it assumes
an accommodation with war, or resignation regarding some "number of sacrificed lives," wherever the sacrifice might occur and for
whatever reason, and as long as peace demands calculations of this
kind, peace is using war as much as it is rejecting it. In opposition to
so many evasions, rebuttals, and so much denial of the fact of violence, and in opposition to so much heedlessness and resignation—
including fatalistic interpretations—the superiority of the night means
first of all restoring to death its absolute nature. The second constitutive element of this superiority is that, given the first point, it alone
is able to accept war as such—that is to say, to entertain no illusions
about peace. Resignation regarding the sacrifice of millions of lives
(in denial of the absoluteness of death) always accompanies what
Patočka calls "demobilization." It consists in imagining that force and
power, where they exist, guarantee that war is a remote possibility—
that war is a peripheral event, inessential and secondary. Finally, the
third element, the ultimate and essential superiority, is that "the night"
alone is able—if not to change or overturn the meaning of the world—
at least to understand it and so to destabilize it. "The night" is inscribed in a logic that is not one of apportionment or partitioning of
force and power, forever unequal and therefore potentially conflic-
tual. Patočka gives a name to this other logic: "the solidarity of the
shaken." All the meditations on history, war, and politics found in
Heretical Essays seem to converge on this concept: "The means by
which this state is overcome is the *solidarity of the shaken*; the solidarity of those who are capable of understanding what life and death are
all about, and so what history is about. That history is the conflict of

mere life, barren and chained by fear, with *life at the peak,* life that does not plan for the ordinary days of a future but sees clearly that the everyday, its life and its 'peace,' have an end. Only one who is able to grasp this, who is capable of conversion, of *metanoia,* is a spiritual person."[17]

What is "life at the peak"? It can only be understood within the context of Patočka's concurrent reflections, as found notably in *Plato and Europe,* on what he calls the "care for the soul," which he will claim in *Heretical Essays* is inseparable from "care for death which becomes the true care for life."[18] "Life at the peak" is that life for which the meaning of the world and the relation to death are inseparable from this care. It grants that "war goes on," because nothing seems to Patočka to be more fragile and threatened than to maintain oneself, precisely, "at the peak"—that is, to persevere in one's elevation. It plumbs the depths—as does Patočka—of the gravity of resignation, renunciation, and compromise, of the petty arrangements with force and power (always fascinating), of great cowardice, and of the dead and burdensome weight of the thousand and one forms of nihilism. Life at the peak is, for all these reasons, "a life in truth."

But this life has no meaning unless it is shared. It can only be lived in the idiomatic invention of the multiple forms of this *other sharing,* forever uncertain, which unsettles the meaning of the world because it apportions the world differently [*parce qu'il fait autrement la part du monde*]. "Life at the peak," the "concern for the soul," and the "care for death" are not the business of one or even of several isolated individuals, locked in heroic resistance against force and power. Patočka's concepts demand first of all a shared understanding, which cannot be reduced to some slogan, or to some facile formula.[19] In this respect, and only in this respect, can they become the cement of the kind of solidarity that transcends all affiliations, a solidarity that cannot be reduced to (or identified with) some profession, some "social class," some party, "nation," or "civilization." Because it is arrayed against the "forces of the day," such solidarity unsettles the terms of the conflict. Into *continuous warfare* [*la guerre continue*] for the apportionment of force and power, the solidarity of the shaken drives the wedge of a different conflict, a different war: the combat that each of us must wage against the confinement of "the meaning of the world" within the ever more exclusive, deadly, and imperious limits of such an apportionment. Patočka claims without hesitation that such solidarity makes the meaning of the world our responsibility, that of each and every one of us. He writes, with a sobriety that has lost none of its relevance:

> The solidarity of the shaken is built up in persecution and uncertainty: that is its front line, quiet, without fanfare or sensation even there where this aspect of the ruling Force seeks to seize it. It does not fear being unpopular but rather seeks it out and calls out quietly, wordlessly. Humankind will not attain peace by devoting and surrendering itself to the criteria of everydayness and of its promises. All who betray this solidarity must realize that they are sustaining war and are the parasites on the sidelines who live off the blood of others. The sacrifices of the front line of the shaken powerfully support this awareness.[20]

5

The Imaginary of Death

≫ PAUL RICŒUR ≪

For Paul Ricœur, as for Sartre, Levinas, Patočka, and Derrida, sections 46 through 53 of *Being and Time,* on the existential analytic of Being-toward-death, constitute one of the most acutely confrontational passages of Heidegger's formidable book. Bearing spirited witness to this is a long passage in part 3 of *Memory, History, Forgetting,* devoted to "the historical condition," in which the philosopher of memory and history considers in his turn the identification of death with "the intimate possibility of one's ownmost potentiality of being," and opposes to it "an alternative reading of the potentiality of dying."[1] However, as Ricœur was writing this book, he was also sketching the outlines of a text titled *Living Up to Death,* each line of which, without taking up Heidegger's analyses explicitly, bears the trace of an engagement with them.[2] The present chapter will focus on these several pages for at least three reasons. First, they foreground what the Heideggerian analytic had discarded from the outset: the tenuous yet forbidding link between the thought of death and the imaginary of death. Second, this link and the attitude toward death that emerges from it invoke a responsibility, both ethical and political, that is incommensurable with the injunction or existential project of an "authentic Being-toward-death." The third reason to examine this text closely is that the ethical and political responsibility invoked cannot be thought without reference to the wars of the twentieth century. The specter of totalitarianism and the extermination of the millions upon millions of people in the concentration camps haunts this text, the memories of which it simultaneously cultivates and orients.

The existential analytic takes no notice of, and expects nothing from, the imaginary of death, of those images of death that grip us or are inflicted on us—any more than it does of those scholarly disciplines that treat such images as their object. At most it presupposes a conceptualization of death that can be elaborated independently of such images. In the worst case it dresses a screen or obstacle before such a conceptualization. This is why such images escape analysis in *Being and Time*—as if it sufficed to show their inauthenticity to reveal the limits of their power, even though we have been *exposed,* from time immemorial, to their recurrent appearances (some would say to their apparitions [*revenance*])—and even though their unfathomable origins constitute the most mysterious, the most obscure part of what we are. All things having a bearing on this imaginary, and the images that compose it have been passed over in silence—not merely the role they might play in the way we envisage our own death as well as that of others, but also the many ways that they were once, and will yet again be put to political use.

Unlike Heidegger, Ricœur begins his meditation on death by commenting on this imaginary. No doubt it is only an outline, the sketch of a book that will forever remain unwritten. But in its pages three kinds of image begin to reveal themselves to our discernment, against which, each and every one, Ricœur will declare himself to be at war. By this very fact these images engage our ethical and political responsibility.

The image of the survivor grips us every time that, as we reflect on death, we imagine the death that we shall become for others. We project ourselves (we survive ourselves) in the gaze and speech of our survivors, like the characters of *No Exit* who are condemned to hear

the commentaries of those who have survived them. We anticipate
with a kind of vertigo the announcement of our dying, the sadness
and the mourning of others, in the hope of "living" as long as possible in their memory, and in anguished expectation of the day when
any trace of our life will have faded away. We wonder what becomes
of us after death, where we will be, what will remain of us in a time
that no longer belongs to us. Death is declined in the future perfect
tense—or, in other words, in the short-circuiting or disregard of the
time that remains to be lived:

> It is tomorrow's death, in the future perfect tense, so to speak, that I
> imagine. And it is this image of the dead person I will be for others
> that takes up all the room, with its load of questions: what are, where
> are, how are the dead?
>
> My struggle is with and against this *image* of tomorrow's dead,
> this dead person that I shall be for the survivors. With and against
> that *make-believe* where death is in some way sucked up by the dead
> person and all the dead.[3]

What is the meaning of this sucking up [*aspiration*] of death by
death and the dead? Why must we, according to Ricœur, combat and
abjure death? Because death, first and most importantly, obscures and
holds in abeyance all that, in thought and in the approach of death,
concerns the part [*partage*] of the living. By imagining in advance
the deceased that I shall become, while attached and clinging to the
various modalities of my survival (which vary from culture to culture), I make the deliberate choice—I decide—to privilege reflection
about what will come *after* (resurrection, reincarnation, hell, or par-
adise) to the detriment of that which *beforehand* (and as long as I am
living) *attaches* me to others. This decision is evidently in conformity with what prevails in writing on the existential analytic of Being-
toward-death. Ricœur, like Heidegger, evacuates from his thinking

both the perspective of survival and any consideration of what comes after death.[4] But unlike Heidegger he does not treat the anticipation [*devancement*] of death as a radical confinement to solitude. His entire thinking is oriented toward that which, in an approach characterized by participation, conducts human relations toward an unsuspected truth. Two dimensions taken together help us discern the outlines of this truth. The first is what Ricœur calls "the coming to light of the Essential,"[5] and the second is "accompanying."[6] As death approaches, both dimensions assume that we must take into consideration before all else "the mobilization of the deepest resources of life to still affirm itself"[7]—and be shared. It is not merely a matter of the relation to death of each of us, but also, as we can readily imagine, of the ethical attitude that is solicited, that is enjoined, by the agony of those who have entered the last phase of their lives.

In this phase, which is always one of trial in the relation that attaches me and binds me to others, whether they be near to me or not so near, reflection on death confronts a second imaginary, the *imaginary of the dying*. This imaginary takes up the greater part of Ricœur's analyses. At stake, in reality, is the configuration of this imaginary, beginning with the way ethical responsibility, whose outlines we are only beginning to discern, is crisscrossed by political implications. Both ethics and politics find in our relation to the imaginary of death one of their most decisive articulations.

The imaginary of the dying relates to the event of death. Ricœur declares himself in a state of war against the imaginary figure of the dying, no less than against the imaginary figure of the survivor: "I am struggling against the make-believe of dying attached to the spectator's gaze for which the suffering person is a dying person; one foresees, one knows with a variable precision that he will soon be dead. It is from this view from the outside on the dying person and the internalized anticipation of this view from the outside on the dying person that I want to deliver myself."[8]

At bottom is the distinction between two terms that ordinary speech often confuses, but which should be kept rigorously distinct if we want to understand anything about the articulation between the person who is in agony and the person who is dying [*l'agonisant et le moribond*]. There is, first of all, the twofold gaze [*double regard*]. There is the gaze that others will direct toward my end, which I can anticipate unto madness as I try to imagine the "almost dead" that I will be for them (one who is dying), for whom there is no hope; and the gaze that I extend toward others as their disappearance nears, as I look upon them as "already dead" because it is the end, because nothing can be done for them and there is *nothing more* to do and perhaps *nothing more* to say. What Ricœur repudiates is first and foremost the placement of these last instants of life under this regime of *nothing more*. In this rejection, moreover, is the meaning and significance of the expression "living unto death" [*vivant jusqu'à la mort*].[9] It restores right [*droit*] to the struggle for life, to the attention, care, and succor that life solicits, in opposition to the pitying [*compatissant*] abandonment, to the measured time, of this confinement to solitude that Norbert Elias has characterized as one of the distinctive traits of modern society.[10] The distinction between agony and dying (a distinction of gaze and attitude) is in this opposition. It is in the recognition of the force, the resources, from which life draws nourishment unto the very end—and to the support that these resources entreat. Ricœur gives the term "accompanying" to the (ethical) responsibility that is engaged by this requirement: "Accompanying is perhaps the most adequate word to designate the favorable attitude thanks to which the gaze directed toward a dying person turns toward him, who is struggling for life until death (note in the margin: understanding + friendship), and not toward a dying person who will soon be dead.

One can speak of sharing despite my reservation concerning the tendency toward fusion or sharing that identifies with the other."[11]

Assuming we would want to adopt this term, we must still ask what is being "shared," what is being *given in common* to him who feels his end is near and to him (or those) by whom he is accompanied. This question points to what is undoubtedly the most decisive attempt to deviate from the path that the existential analytic of Being-toward-death had consistently followed in its engagement with all thinking about dying. The author of *Living Up to Death* offers a response to this question that recalls, further upstream, the concept of sharing toward which Plato advances in *Phaedo*. Sharing, Plato says, is about the emergence of the essential, or the "inner grace" that knows no attachment [*appartenance*]. In similar fashion, the essential, which Ricœur describes as a movement of transcendence, will also serve as the term around which his entire meditation will be articulated. But why speak of deviating? What is this essential? And what is being transcended?

If Ricœur deviates from the beaten path of the existential analytic, it is above all because the approach of death and the thought of death are placed under the sign of a *sharing*—of an experience of friendship and fraternity, incommensurable with any form of heroic solitude. The question is not "How to relate, without diversion, ruse, or distraction, to my ownmost possibility—the possibility of my own impossibility?" but rather "With whom (accompanied by what friends, what family) shall I die?"

If the imaginary of the survivor and the dying are both rejected, it is because they definitively compromise this dimension of friendship and fraternity. In a text titled "La mort," Ricœur brings a greater degree of precision to this dual dimension. The essential, the fundamental, he explains, concerns *the transfer of the love of life to the other*. Friendship and fraternity assume detachment from the self, an openness to this transfer, which remains impossible as long as one is under the sway of these two imaginaries. Whether I imagine myself as either a survivor or at the threshold of death, in neither construction is anything being shared. On the contrary, all forms of *attachment to self* (the cords that entwine life) are being allowed to proliferate. Haunted by the images of survival, or by those of the destiny of the dead, we are unable to imagine that there is something to give or to receive: "The relation between openness to the essential, for the fundamental, and the transfer to others who will survive me is reciprocal: openness for the fundamental, freed up by 'detachment,' *founds* the transfer—the transfer *verifies, attests, tests,* the 'test' of detachment in its dimension of generosity."[12]

Ricœur explains that this movement of transcendence surpasses by right all forms of belonging, that it resists absorption by cultural, religious, social, or economic and political difference, and indeed any kind of difference. If the transfer knows no frontiers it is because agony has the effect of dismantling them—otherwise it would be senseless to speak of the *essential* or the *fundamental*. What these words signify is that in the face of death, whether one's own or that of others, in the time of agony, when life's "deepest resources" still mobilize behind it, *nothing, absolutely nothing,* no consideration of whatever magnitude, must—on one side or the other—constrain, limit, or interfere with the *transfer* of the love of life.

We must therefore keep the following distinction in mind. The person in agony is the person to whom we recognize the right to share, until the very end ("living unto death"—this is the meaning of *accompanying*), whereas inversely, as soon as he is looked on as a person who is dying, he is denied this right—it is confiscated. He is precipitously cast over into life's beyond. But a question arises. There is no doubt that this sharing, this transfer, concerns those—first and foremost—who are close to the agonizing person. Ricœur does not place them under the sign of understanding and friendship in vain. But what of the others? Does this distinction between agony and dying cease to be meaningful beyond the circle of close friends and family? Does not the movement of transcendence invite us to enlarge the sphere of our responsibility—to conceive it as political responsibility?

Ricœur does not ignore the political dimension of the relation to death, as evidenced by his response, in an interview with Marc de Launay and François Azouvi, to a question regarding the development of totalitarianism in the twentieth century. Ricœur offers this comment on Jorge Semprún's epigraph to *Literature and Life,* which states, "I am searching for the crucial region of the soul where absolute Evil confronts fraternity":

> It is, therefore, not by accident that totalitarianism resulted in extermination, that is to say, the infliction of mass death: through the destruction of interhuman bonds, humanity becomes a *massa perdita,* in which the moribund and the dead are almost indistinguishable. . . .
>
> Is this not where the essence of totalitarianism is to be found, in the *institutional* extermination made possible by the elimination of everything that organically formed the social fabric? *Mass deaths* are the sign or the index of the exterminating character proper to the totalitarian regime; they testify to the fact that death is not an accident but the step-by-step contamination of those who are already dead in the direction of the moribund. There is, at the very source of totalitarianism, a proliferating experience of death.[13]

Totalitarianism at its core, however, is not only the institutional organization of extermination, but the habituation of the gaze to perceive, if not to "treat," a part of humanity as a *massa perdita* by organizing the contagious spread of the idea that those who are already dead and those who are condemned to die are somehow "glued" together. At stake is humanity's resignation, humanity's *eclipse.* The distinction between the person "in agony" and the person "who is dying" has a political dimension, because when we accept in one way or another that such or such a "population," globally, wherever it might be, is perceived as already dead, when we expunge the fact of existence of thousands of men and women while they still live, it is this "humanity," which Ricœur places under the sign of fraternity, that is irremediably compromised. If it is true that there is a political dividing line between two ways of perceiving the event of death, then we must ask ourselves at what moment and with regard to what frontiers, to what economic, cultural, or geopolitical demarcations, are those who agonize now perceived to be dying, and thus merged in a *massa perdita* in which all distinction is lost. Ricœur, with this question, introduces a third configuration in his combat against the imaginary of death: the personification of death.

Ricœur links this image very explicitly to the amalgamation [*confusion*] that characterizes the *massa perdita*: "I would be inclined to believe that personified, active, destructive death enters make-believe at the point where the already dead dead and those dying people who will soon be dead become indistinct."[14]

Ricœur questions how, as death is placed under the sign of absolute evil, the agonizing and the dying become identified with one another and are personified. Personification raises the risk that any reflection on death will be engulfed by the memory of extermination, that any death, in other words, will be assimilated with the violence exercised by some absolute evil—and that death will thus become more real than life. All life is thus exposed to death as enduring threat; all life is haunted by the memory of violent death, with the result that all humanity is fused ahead of time and forever more with a *massa perdita* that is "catalyzed" by evil.[15] Rather than "living unto death," as Ricœur would hope, we would forever be "survivors" in a world foreign to all hope of fraternity. It would be futile to try to minimize the power of this third imaginary. Our relation to death, as to history, would not be able to elude its ghostly allure [*hantise*]. In the imaginary of death personified we see the outlines of a profligate culture that, while not without legitimacy, can sometimes confine us in a chilling fascination with *Death* (capitalized) and *Evil* (capitalized), often magnified and reinforced by a bewildering abundance of images and evocations of violent death, real and virtual, foisted on us day after day by newspapers, magazines, television, cinema, video games, and so forth.[16] Death and evil become confounded in a powerful imaginary that challenges fraternity. The imaginary is so imposing and so routine that, contrary to the political instrumentalization of the relation to death and of the memory of the dead, it turns the expression "living unto death," if not into a program, at least into a challenge for thought:

> With this, a difficult road opens: if absolute Evil goes hand in hand with fraternity, mourning must pass through the exorcism of the phantoms generated by absolute Evil starting from the rot of the *massa perdita* where the dying and the cadavers are brought together in their power of pestilential contagion. . . .
>
> My problem is born from this: in what condition is ordinary death itself contaminated by death at the limit, *horrible* death? And how to struggle against this counterfeit?[17]

Ricœur pursued this challenge relentlessly. It is probable that his great work, *Memory, History, Forgetting,* among others, was written in response to this exigency. There can be no "good use of the memory of death" (i.e., a memory freed from the three imaginaries examined here) without mourning—mourning whose mainstay (the mainstay of fraternity) is the narrative of those who returned and who "have made life prevail over the 'memory of the death.'"[18] Thought must therefore turn, in the end, to this twofold task of remembering and mourning, inseparably joined together. Ricœur sets thought in motion toward this truth, regarding whose pursuit he says, in a concluding sentence, "Yes, reach the point where the *truth* that expels the phantoms is this: the eternal struggle between fraternity and absolute Evil."[19]

6

Fraternity and Absolute Evil

> I seek the crucial region of the soul where absolute Evil and
> fraternity clash.
>
> —ANDRÉ MALRAUX, *Miroir des Limbes*

This declaration from André Malraux's *Miroir des Limbes* has a long
history. Jorge Semprún used it as the epigraph of *Literature or Life,*
which narrates his deportation to Buchenwald in the last year of the
war and his "return to life." Paul Ricœur, who had read Semprún's book
(published in 1994), reprised Malraux's declaration, as we saw, in
Living Up to Death. Neither author assumes the risk of explicitly locat-
ing the "region of the soul" that Malraux seeks to reveal, the region
where the antagonism between absolute evil and fraternity takes root
and is decided. But because all these authors are haunted by the memory of the wars and the extermination camps of the twentieth century,
they all indicate that this antagonism can only be addressed from the
perspective of reflections stimulated by that war and the Holocaust,
in two different registers, regarding an "apportionment" [*partage*] of
death. The experience both of absolute evil and of fraternity, bound
together both by what unites them and by what opposes them, occurs,
they tell us, in the proximity of death—not so much in the relation
that one cultivates with regard to the possibility of one's own disappearance, as Being-toward-death (authentic or not), but rather in one's
singular relation to the death of the other.

For a difficulty arises immediately regarding this relation. Are the
"other" and one's "brothers" one and the same? Or, on the contrary,
are not the death of the other and the death of one's "brothers" two

trials whose radical separation, disjunction, or delimitation (perhaps encouraged or sought by politics, religion, or ideology) enables the irruption of evil? The memory of war in the twentieth century is that of a great multitude of murders committed *in the name* of brothers and their fraternity, in their defense, for their preservation, for their salvation. It is also the memory of the various perverse transformations of fraternity into hostility and even into absolute hostility. That memory teaches us, through scores of eyewitness accounts and narratives, how fragile are the bonds of brotherhood and how easily yesterday's brothers can become tomorrow's enemies, and how much that about-face forever signifies the irreducible possibility of putting the other to death. The fragility of brotherhood, and the ease with which it is subverted, are perhaps themselves one of the forms and manifestations of evil. Therefore one cannot escape, on the one hand, the solipsism of a singular relation to death, one that is *perhaps blind to evil,* without turning our attention to the words and gestures of care and assistance that open death up to *a fraternal sharing.* On the other hand, however, it is from the very heart of fraternity, from the way it is circumscribed and exclusive, and from the frontiers, real or symbolic, which run through it, that evil can irrupt. Malraux's "search" therefore points to an *aporia.* Our reflection in this chapter seeks, as far as possible, to bring the terms of this aporia into greater proximity.

At the start of his narrative, Semprún tells us of two inextricably entangled aspects of the time he spent in Buchenwald. The first is that it was, day in and day out, a journey through death and with death: "I'm struck by the idea, if one can call it an idea (that tonic flash of warmth, that rush of blood, that pride in the bodily knowledge of something vital), struck by the sudden overwhelming feeling, in any case, that I have not escaped death, but passed through it. Rather it passed through me. That I have in a way, lived through it. That I have come back from it the way you return from a voyage that has transformed and—perhaps—transfigured you."[1]

The second is that this passage was not accomplished without a sharing, inscribed in the help and support of "fraternal" gestures, words, and glances, exchanged *in the face* of death, and *in opposition to* [*contre*] death—to its destitution, its division, and its isolation: "For almost two years, I'd seen a fraternal spirit gleaming in the eyes of those around me—when the light in their eyes hadn't gone out altogether. Most of the deportees had dead eyes. Their gaze had been clouded, extinguished, blinded by the crude glare of death. . . . But whatever light still survived in their gaze was a fraternal one. From being nourished on so much death probably. Nourished on such huge portions [*Nourri d'un si riche partage*]."[2]

Fraternity is thus presented, exemplified, as the experience of a relation to death that gathers and unites rather than separates. It does so first in the ordeal of that accompanying the dying that held Ricœur's attention as he read, among other passages, Semprún's narrative of Maurice Halbwachs's last days.[3] Conceptualized as *care for the other* and *attentiveness toward the other,* fraternity consists in not abandoning the dying to their own solitude before death—to the solitude that would *erase* fraternity by deleting [*exceptant*] the dying from the world of the living prior to their disappearance. Fraternity establishes a *common* front against death, characterized first of all by the refusal to allow the other (the brother), out of resignation, to die— to let him die as if there were *already* nothing more to expect of him or to offer him.[4] Because such a refusal always solicits a last word, a last look, a last smile, it allows the dying, Ricœur writes, to "remain living unto death." "Dying, he would smile, fixing his eyes on me like a brother," Semprún writes and reiterates several times.[5] In the extreme circumstances of the two years spent in the Buchenwald camp, described in his narrative, the singularity of this "accompanying" is, at least for some of the internees, its *reciprocity*. The front against death is a *common* front because its "experience," which is simultaneously an experience of radical evil, is collective, and because that experience founds, if not a singular being-together, at least a "being-with" that Semprún (who discovered Heidegger before the war, thanks to Levinas's first publications) has no hesitation in calling a "Mit-Sein-zum-Tode" (being-with-toward-death).[6]

However elliptic, this evocation of Being-toward-death provokes two reactions, of which each would require an endless number of developments and nuances, given the many questions they suggest when read beside such eyewitness accounts and narratives as those of Primo Levi, Robert Antelme, Elie Wiesel, Charlotte Delbo, and so many others. The first reaction is this: assuming one would want to turn "fraternity" into an ethical and political category, the bi-dimensionality of the experience of radical evil is revealed first and foremost in what we will have to call, at least provisionally, "the experience of death"—an experience that is not merely the anxious anticipation that each of us could or should have regarding our own impossibility, but also a defense, a resistance, and an apprehension that is commonly held. Because death is ubiquitous and menacing, and because nothing more can protect us against it, it reveals, in (fragile) outline, the delineation of a "community" that is both ethical and political, simultaneously. It is ethical in that it refuses or tends to refuse, *to the extent that it can*—and in defiance against all the forces that oppose it (planning and organizing terror)—that the imminence of death, in its barest nakedness, and the fear that it breeds, should shake, break up, and finally destroy the "moral relations" that continue to constitute, *at the limits of the possible,* the fabric of existence. It is political to the extent that it embodies, for as long as this possibility remains open to it, an irreducible opposition to the forever murderous desire to *shackle each and every one separately to the conditions of his or her own survival.*

The second reaction is this: that one element of the destructive obstruction of *fraternity* by evil may simultaneously have been brought to light. In reading eyewitness accounts and narratives it becomes clear that the malnutrition, the exhaustion by hard labor, the deprivations, the blows, the threats, the executions, the random violence, all pursued the goal of *absolute separation,* by fixating and blinding the lives of each inmate to the impossible satisfaction of those needs that "survival" requires. Every component of terror helped to blunt, and even to suspend and destroy, the possibility of moral and ethical relations, to reduce to their barest extreme the time and the space—the time and space of fraternity—that could be assigned to such relations.

As we emphasized at the beginning of this chapter, neither Semprún nor Ricœur nor even Malraux is able to tell us, explicitly and definitively, how absolute evil opposes fraternity. But the preceding analyses already help us understand why this opposition cannot be conceptualized independently of a singular relation to *the death of the other.* They insinuate, like a kind of photographic negative, that evil will remain beyond our grasp and comprehension for as long as we fail to shed light on how some or other feature of *fraternity in the face of death and against death* is forever being eclipsed and suspended, or denied and in the end even suppressed. The preceding analyses show us that evil is at work at the heart of moral and political relations in at least two ways. It manifests itself on the one hand as violation and perversion, and on the other hand as accommodation [*compromission*] and the destruction of a "sharing of death." We must take this twofold manifestation into consideration if we want to understand how evil engages not only the relations between the executioners and their victims, but also the relations that the victims are compelled and reduced to adopt toward one another. Regarding the latter, no eyewitness account of "survival" in the concentration camps fails to relate the relentless efforts of the SS to wipe out completely any expectation or hope of help *in the face* of death and *against* death. For many internees—those who at Auschwitz were designated by the term "Muslims"—there was, as Primo Levi, Jean Améry, and Bruno Bettelheim all reveal, no sharing, no exchange, no help possible as death approached.[7] The uncertain frontier between survival and death became clouded, indiscernible. The "Muslims" (the majority of internees) no longer belonged to the world of the living—to that world that still invites the gestures, words, and glances that are soliciting help. *Before having left life,* they are excluded from life, turned back from it, reduced to the state of an "anonymous mass" by the stress of inhuman living conditions. Because the approach of death, its apprehension, its threat can no longer be shared, and because the internees no longer ask for nor expect anything from anyone, one hesitates, as Primo Levi makes clear, to "call their death death":

> Their life is short, but their number is endless; they, the *Muselmänner,* the drowned, form the backbone of the camp, an anonymous mass, continually renewed and always identical, of non-men who march and labor in silence, the divine spark dead within them, already too empty to really suffer. One hesitates to call them living: *one hesitates to call their death death, in the face of which they have no fear, as they are too tired to understand.*
>
> They crowd my memory with their faceless presences, and if I could enclose *all the evil of our time* in one image, I would choose this image which is familiar to me: an emaciated man, with head dropped and shoulders curved, on whose face and in whose eyes not a trace of a thought is to be seen.[8]

The "faceless presence" of these anonymous masses, avoiding one another's gaze—Ricœur's *massa perdita*—haunts the history of the last century. It summarizes—*yesterday as well as today*—"all the evil of our times," and evokes a thousand and one eyewitness accounts. The singularity of the Nazi extermination camps is no doubt a fact without parallel, a historical fracture. But the "Being-in-the-world" of "lost masses," of "moribund populations," banished from one frontier to the next, exposed to famine, to epidemics, to terror, to political violence, to the fluctuating combat zones of unending warfare (and the many refugee camps that fluctuate with them), deprived of any assistance, will have survived the disappearance of the camps. If it is true that these masses are *today* one of the faces assumed by exclusion, basically everywhere in a world from which they are deleted [*exceptés*] *in advance* (because there is no room for them), and from which they are condemned in advance to disappear, without a trace, then we must ask if the *relation* signified by their abandonment to this anticipated and anonymous death is not inscribed in this kind of *summary account.*[9]

But evil, as we said above, also engages with the relation of the executioners to the death of their victims. It presupposes that the latter are not (or are no longer) either heard or seen as "possible brothers"—and that by this account their death is therefore not *real* death, that it is neither conceived or experienced and certainly not shared *as the death of the other,* that it no longer elicits either their support or their accompanying. Every crime—and especially mass crimes, crimes against humanity and war crimes—every genocide presupposes that an exception must be made to the solicitude, to the compassion, that death evokes (not mine, but that of *every other*). It is *decided* in advance that some part of humanity, some determinate group of individuals, will not be able to "remain living unto death," and thus not be entitled to help, because they are already dead, not only destined and condemned to disappear, but in reality already passed from view, wiped from the map as if their lives, effectively suppressed, could not make a difference to anyone. Evil in this case is nothing more than the methodical will to realize this "deletion" [*exception*]. Evil efficiently

goes about organizing the disappearance of those for whom no solicitude is asked or hoped for. By suspending fraternity for some category of individuals (a "people," an "ethnic group," a "social class"), *in
the face of* and *against* death, evil *cleaves* the imaginary of dying into
two irreducible parts by imposing on all, through terror and propaganda, a partition among the living. Evil traces a line of division [*ligne
de partage*], an irreducible *frontier* that delimits two radically heterogeneous ways (this is the meaning of radical evil) of anticipating the
death of *some* other. Evil is nourished and increased by the separation between the lives of those who still count (those who have value
or worth) and the lives of those that *already* count for nothing (the
lives that we are told, through statements, declarations, bombast, and
bellowing, are all but worthless).

The difficulty thus arises entirely from the fact that, conceptualized
in these terms, the opposition between evil and fraternity places us,
from the start, before an aporia. If it is true that evil separates and
divides those whose death *affects us* (because it elicits compassion and
lends itself to mourning) from those regarding whom some ideology, policy, propaganda, or exhortation to murder have determined
that their death does not affect us—from those, in other words, who
in one form or another, and for some reason or another, will have
been deleted in advance from the world of the living—it is also true
that this separation is not foreign to the recognition, or to the construction, imagination, promotion, exaltation (even unto murderous
intoxication), of some or other fraternal bond. Is it not always something like fraternity that *distinguishes* (in all senses of the term) those
who can be recognized and "protected" as brothers from the others,
from all others who, for reasons of "race," "ethnicity," "origin," language, religion (or some other form of belonging), cannot or can no
longer be so recognized? Assuming that evil cannot, and does not

allow itself to be conceptualized independently of this denial of the gestures, glances, or utterances that can elicit help—that is to say, that are fraternal—it might be the case, putting it another way (and this is the meaning of the aporia), that it is from fraternity itself that this denial proceeds. Everything that is predisposed to bring people together and unite them in a shared relation to death, a being-together-in-the-face-of-death (a fraternity, camaraderie, community, or solidarity), has as its downside [*revers*]—a downside that is perhaps at the origin of evil—to immediately exclude, discriminate, mark the difference between those deaths that count (that touch *us*, that affect *us* and *bereave* us) and those whom we know, or about whom it has been decided in advance and about whom we have received instruction, that they will not count, or will count only as the elements of some macabre bookkeeping. There is doubtless no war, and certainly no war crime or crime against humanity, that does not imply this kind of partition, and that does not depend on the means that are mobilized (propaganda or terror) to make this partition appear self-evident.

There is no "fraternization," camaraderie, whether affecting [*affectante*] or affected [*affecté*], that does not cast the shadow of some murder that may have been committed in its name. It presupposes pledges, oaths, and promises—the promise, for example, to share in the mourning of brothers or "friends" who have disappeared, but also to avenge them—which turn expeditiously against those who might constitute a threat to the bonds that tie brothers together, whether natural or constructed.

There is a risk of confusion here, and it should be avoided. Not all "fraternities" are of equal worth. One cannot give like treatment to the fraternity of victims and the fraternity of executioners. Brotherhood in the first instance means the help and support that is shared and reciprocal in the face of imminent death. In the second instance it means an exclusion, a deletion, whose consequence for the Jews of Europe was their confinement in ghettos, followed by their murder and extermination. True, the gestures, the glances, the utterances connoted by the fraternity of victims are radically heterogeneous when compared with the brutality and the violence that is always signified by the fraternity of the executioners. But the word's ambivalence (wherein the terms of the aporia are located) reminds us that every time we speak of "fraternity" we have to grasp it in its twofold meaning. On the one hand, it designates a mode of being of the relation to the other that is in opposition (though not securely) to indifference and hostility. To be fraternal, to "fraternize," implies putting down one's arms (at least for a time), showing goodwill, pledging alliance, and sharing in the joys and sufferings of the other. On the other hand, it supposes circumscription, limits, and frontiers. It traces a line of *division* (and we note that the same term, the same semantic register, is always used: part, partition, apportionment) between brothers (whether brothers by "nature" or by decree) and the other. In other words, the term "brothers" is itself divided if not torn between a mode of "being-with-the-other" and a particular modality of "being-together"—of "the we." And if we speak here of being torn, it is because neither of the two meanings, despite their heterogeneity (between that of being-with-the-other and that of "being-together"), can be conceptualized without contamination by the other. As long as "being-with-the-other," in this modality, proclaims an alliance or an attachment, it implies the possibility of an about-face [*revirement*], of a conversion [*retournement*] of fraternity into hostility: expulsion, purification, divorce. Circumscribing the being-together is never accomplished without the *appropriation* of fraternal gestures and words. It retains and promises them, it reserves them, for "the we" that it opposes to one or more "them's" against whom there is no ruling out that they will mobilize and arm themselves. The *sharing of death* is thus understood in two ways that are not easily dissociated and yet between which it is imperative that we draw a distinction. Is it not the meaning of the aporia that this impossible distinction is necessary? Is this not evil's place of origin?

But Malraux's phrase, "I seek the crucial region of the soul where absolute Evil and fraternity clash," and its citation by Semprún and Ricœur nevertheless hold out the possibility that fraternity might be understood in yet a *third sense*. We saw above that this clash between evil and fraternity is not self-evident, for example when absolute evil, understood in its radicality, emerges from a fraternal relationship, understood in turn as the circumscription of an exclusive and, as such, potentially deadly "being-together." This circumscription, this delimitation of frontiers (cultural, linguistic, ethnic, racial, or other), in other words, always assumes that the designation of the enemy is variable, modifiable, and manipulable, and always assumes that it can be indifferently designated as within or without, giving rise, for example, to a fraternal enmity [*frères ennemis*]. Unless ... unless fraternity lets itself be conceptualized as the regulatory idea of a *universal fraternity*—a fraternity whose help and support, gestures, words, and gaze, *addressed to all,* without calculation (strategic, geopolitical, economic, or ideological), were to transcend all belonging, foreign [*étranger*] to the diversity of "origins," cultures, languages, or religions. Is this what enables the evil that, proceeding from fraternity, becomes hostile to fraternity? Would this evil be nothing more than the denial of such a universality or, even more menacing, its confiscation, its withdrawal inside a particular *exemplification*?

Regarding this necessary ideal of universal brotherhood, Derrida reminds us in *The Politics of Friendship* that its invocation, its solicitation, in every instance in which it has been translated (historically) into fact, has only been translated through the language of some nation (or through some other determinant particularity) according to the logic of its exemplarity.[10] As was the case during the French Revolution, the idea of a universal brotherhood is accompanied, more often than not, by an apportionment, by a partition (yet another one) between those who declare their readiness to shoulder the burden of fraternity, to embody it, but who turn it into the sign of their *election,* and all others regarding whom the decision was made in advance, unilaterally, that fraternization would require certain preliminary conditions—in other words, that the others be teachable, and instructed in and won to the fraternity, by force, violence, or terror, if necessary. However universal its claims might be, fraternity *in this sense* falls prey to arguments developed by Franz Rosenzweig in response to his friend Rosenstock's efforts to convert him to Christianity (in their 1916 correspondence, which Rosenzweig would later reveal in *The Star of Redemption*). For Rosenzweig the idea of *election* had long ago been transformed into the "color enhancement of all the nationalities," on some or other field of battle over which nations were contending (and, one should add, are still contending) in order to win or impose (notably by force of arms) the recognition of the nation's claims to embody not merely a chosen people but also a universal mission, with which a people believed itself to have been invested.[11]

Regarding this third and last understanding of "fraternity" (as the regulatory idea of a universal fraternity), one must once again acknowledge that its power to oppose absolute evil is tenuous. One encounters the same orchestration of the death of the other, now perpetrated in the name of *universal fraternity,* which can be demanded in the name of a universal history, depicted more often than not as a law of historical progress. The universality of fraternity, in other words, is never without *deletion.* Revolutionary terror has always brandished fraternity as its justification, above all when those revolutions declared their commitment to "friendship among the peoples" (*druzhba narodov*) so as to warrant their policies of purification and homogenization, as well as their right to conquest and their expansionist ambitions.

We can deduce an axiom from the foregoing analysis: whenever the frontiers become blurred, the fragility of fraternity's resistance to evil derives from one and the same principle—which is, first and fore-most, the principle of an *eclipse, the eclipse of the relation to the death of the other,* which should be serving as the foundation of fraternity. If it is true, as I have tried to show, that fraternity, from the beginning, is perverted every time an exception is made to the ethical and polit-ical imperative (as regards speech and action) of a *common front against death,* and if it is perverted every time that—for whatever reason, motive, indifference, or madness—*putting-to-death or allowing-to-die* prevails over this common front, then it is *this relation that must be rethought.*

As Derrida taught us to think, through numerous texts, notably in "Rams" and *The Work of Mourning,* it is friendship [*amitié*], more than fraternity [*fraternité*], that conveys the meaning of this relation to death. The death of a friend, he writes, always signifies "the end of the world":

> For each time, and each time singularly, each time irreplaceably, each time infinitely, death is nothing less than an end of *the* world. Not *only one* end among others, the end of someone or of some-thing *in the world,* the end of a life or of a living being. Death puts an end neither to someone in the world nor to *one* world among oth-ers. Death marks each time, each time in defiance of arithmetic, the absolute end of the one and only world, of that which each opens as a one and only world, the end of the unique world, the end of the totality of what is or can be presented as the origin of the world for any unique living being, be it human or not.[12]

In an earlier text, in which he subjects to detailed analysis the exis-tential analytic of Being-toward-death (as deployed in paragraphs 46–53 of *Being and Time,* discussed in chapter 1), Derrida insists on the fact that Heidegger, in his thematization of the relation to death, fails to mention or even to acknowledge mourning.[13] Mourning enters into consideration only to the extent that it might affect or perturb Being-in-the-world. While making this observation, Derrida surmises that the consideration of mourning (though missing in Heidegger's text) might well supply a political dimension that invites interrogation. We must therefore ask what this politics of mourning, or some or other politics of memory, might consist of—how, for example, it might concern itself with what I am trying to argue here regarding the clash between absolute evil and fraternity.

To the deaths regarding which it has been decided, foreseen, or simply accepted or tolerated that they do not count [*compter*]—to the *abstract deaths of the world,* to the deaths heaped in advance into an anonymous mass (Ricœur's *massa perdita*), the possibility to signify, *by each death singularly,* and for anyone living, *the end of the world,* is refused, denied, or forbidden. Absolute evil's campaigns of destruction have no other goal than to consign the signification of the deaths of its victims to oblivion—to make us forget, everywhere and always, that death is indeed "the end of the world." This forgetting, however, does not happen after the deaths of the victims. It is not tied to memory's flaws, but, on the contrary, is anticipated and prefigured in the calculations and in the organization of mass murder. It is foreseen in the executions and disappearances of those for whom, for this very reason, death will not have been death. No war crime, no crime against humanity, no genocide has ever occurred without the attempt to orchestrate this forgetting—by trying to wipe away all trace of the crime, or by trying to dispose of the bodies. Absolute evil opposes fraternity (as the help and care that are enjoined by the death of the other) in so far as it tries to deny a part of humanity, condemned to an anonymous death, the mourning that is its due.

7

Hospitality and Mortality

⤜ JACQUES DERRIDA ⤛

> For hospitality is not simply some region of ethics, let alone, and
> we will return to this, the name of a problem in law or politics: it is
> ethicity itself, the whole and the principle of ethics.
>
> —JACQUES DERRIDA, *Adieu to Emmanuel Levinas*

> But if *I must* (and this is ethics itself) carry the other in me in order
> to be faithful to him, in order to respect his singular alterity, a
> certain melancholy must still protest against normal mourning.
>
> —JACQUES DERRIDA, *Sovereignties in Question: The Poetics of Paul Celan*

This epigraph in two parts establishes hospitality and mourning as
the principle of ethics. The word "itself" [*même*] designates both the
one and the other as the essence of ethics. How are we to understand
this conjunction? Does it mean that one of the two terms (hospitality) concerns our relation to the living and the other (mourning) our
memory of the dead? Or, on the contrary, should we not say instead
that the one term cannot be conceptualized without the other? And,
if this is so, what does this impossible dissociation of the twofold
responsibility that is being implied teach us about death itself—about
our own mortality and that of others? Assuming that hospitality is
"all of ethics," how is mourning inscribed in this "all"? And how do
the one and the other affect one's relation to oneself, indeed the very
idea of one*self* [*soi*], of one's place [*chez soi*], or of one's identity as
self [*identité à soi*]?

One could doubtlessly start by showing how questions such as these are constantly haunting Derrida's thinking. It would not be difficult to follow the trace of such questions, beginning with the quotation from Edgar Allan Poe that Derrida places in the epigraph of *The Voice and the Phenomenon,* and continuing up through his final interview with *Le Monde* (in the summer of 2004)[1]—paying particular attention to the many works that he dedicated to the memory of friends who passed away.[2] Such questions are forever orienting his engagement with works to which he returns repeatedly and frequently, as if, in the mystery [*secret*] of the conjunction between hospitality and mourning, these same questions contained the key to their singular articulation. This is as true of his reading of *Being and Time* as it is of the attention he pays, in *Aporias,* to the existential analytic of Being-toward-death, and more precisely to the reluctance, apparent in that analytic, to evoke the responsibility of mourning. It is no less true of his readings of Freud (his *Metapsychology*), of the poems of Celan, most notably in "Rams: Uninterrupted Dialogue," of the narratives of Blanchot in *Parages* and *Demeure,* and of the theoretical writings of Paul de Man in *Memoires for Paul de Man*. Finally, it is this two-pronged question regarding hospitality and mortality (both mine and the other's) that situates the culmination of his "architectonic" confrontation with the works of Emmanuel Levinas.

How do the questions of mourning and hospitality relate to each other? To answer this question we need first to understand what makes the relation to the death of the other the essence of ethics ("ethics itself"), in the sense that it governs indissociably both the relation to self and the relation to others. Whatever form might be given to ethics, whatever heritage we might affirm, we commonly conceptualize ethics as something that concerns primarily the relation of each of us singly to the whole of all living beings. Mourning and the rules that govern the way that one (with other living beings) partakes [*partage*] in it are understood, at best, as a limited part of those relations to which ethics in its totality applies. Derrida seeks—in works that include his reading of Freud's analysis of the work of mourning—to carry out an initial, radical displacement by deconstructing that which, within ethics, disconnects our relation to the living from our memory of the dead. In effect, that separation always presupposes, first and foremost, an I that is identical to itself, such that the relation to others (living and dead) only affects it outwardly, haphazardly, and secondarily. The I can distinguish what it owes to the living from what it owes to the dead only to the extent that it is assured of what it owes to itself independently of the others, no matter the name (autonomy, sovereignty, etc.) that one might give to this assurance. Therefore, in order to effect a displacement, this assurance must be shaken. Everything changes, everything should change, when we recognize—what one calls deconstruction has no object if not this—that the I exists only as affected by the trace of the other in the I, and that this is the meaning of finitude.

This trace, Derrida tells us, is always already mourning. It is even *originarily* mourning, if we are willing to acknowledge that the experience of the other is inseparable from the experience of the possibility of the other's disappearance, and thus precedes, *by this very fact,* the incurred obligation to conserve the memory of the other. Derrida, in *Memoires for Paul de Man,* recalls us decisively to this realization:

> The "me" or the "us" of which we speak then arise and are delimited in the way that they are only through this experience of the other, and of the other as other who can die, leaving in me or in us this memory of the other. This terrible solitude which is mine or ours at the death of the other is what constitutes that relationship to self which we call "me," "us," "between us," "subjectivity," "intersubjectivity," "memory." The *possibility* of death "happens," so to speak, "before" these different instances, and makes them possible. . . . We

know, we knew, *we remember*—before the death of the loved one—
that being-in-me or being-in-us is constituted out of the possibility
of mourning. We are only ourselves from the perspective of this
knowledge that is older than ourselves; and this is why I say that we
begin by *recalling* this to ourselves: we come to ourselves through
this memory of *possible* mourning.[3]

We can now better understand how mourning concerns not only
the memory that we retain of the dead, but also our relation to the
living. It affects the trace that the living leave behind in us, in the very
place where our "identity" is disjointed, open and disposed toward
alterity—that is to say, nonidentical. Mourning affects the trace because there is no living being for which we can determine, by decree,
in advance, that we will not some day have to preserve its memory.
However, two questions immediately arise. The first concerns the very
possibility of such mourning. In his critical discussion of Freud's
analyses in *On Metapsychology,* and in his reading of the works of Abraham and Torok, Derrida reminds us again and again that if mourning
is "ethics itself," it is because, first and foremost—and in conformity
with what gives ethics its hyperbolic, that is, its aporetic character—
it *affirms the impossible*.[4] The law of mourning demands in effect that
we retain the memory of the other. But, at the very moment at which
we commit to *its* interiorization, the law of mourning places limits on
that interiorization. The other, we know, is always larger than our
memory of it. The other exceeds the words and the images that we
associate with its memory. For this reason we can never be done with
the other [*nous n'en avons jamais fini avec lui*]. Unlike Freud, for
whom mourning consists in retaining the other in the self, in bearing
its world, Derrida emphasizes over and over again the aporetic character of such a "preservation." The "idealizing introjection" that is normalized by [*que norment*] Freud's analyses does not measure up to
the other's alterity. It does not allow (or no longer allows) the other

to appear as other. Such is, moreover, the meaning of the assertion, found in "Rams: Uninterrupted Dialogue," and reprised here in the epigraph: the ethics of mourning demands melancholy because, in opposition to all codifications and normalizations, melancholy alone assumes the *possibility of the impossible*. The *hyperbole* of ethics resides in this assumption.

To say therefore that the anticipation of mourning, understood as possibility of the impossible, structures every relation to the other—to the living other—means that there is no identity to self, there is no being self, no being in one's self's place, that is not put in question by this hyperbole. We all know, as surely as we know our own finitude, that we may have to bear the burden of an impossible memory—of a memory that will not, that cannot, measure up to the other: "Upon the death of the other we are given to memory, and thus to interiorization, since the other, outside us, is now nothing. And with the dark light of this nothing, we learn that the other resists the closure of our interiorizing memory. With the nothing of this irrevocable absence, the other appears *as* other, and as other for us, upon his death, since death constitutes and makes manifest the limits of a *me* or an *us* who are obliged to harbor something that is greater and other than them; something *outside of them within them*."[5]

The second question that arises concerns how far this relation extends. In most of the works that Derrida devotes to mourning he discusses the memory of friends who have passed away, or the anticipation of their possible disappearance amid friendship. We find the crux of his thinking in three works: the book he dedicated to the memory of Paul de Man, in his tribute to Hans-Georg Gadamer, and in *The Work of Mourning*. But ethics (*ethics itself*) does not only concern friends. It is not even certain that it can be limited to human beings, or even to living beings with which we, each of us, are in relation. We only arrive at ourselves, Derrida tells us, from the lived possibility, as "terrible experience,"[6] of the death of the other. But what is the other (what is the other living being) regarding whom we can decide, in advance, that there will be or can be no relation? For whom can we decree that his or her disappearance shall remain remote? If mourning is hyperbolical, it is not merely because of its impossible necessity but also because, by right [*en droit*], its anticipation cannot be circumscribed so as to encompass only some group or determinate category of individuals. Apart from his indeterminate usage of the first person plural, there are few indications in Derrida's texts concerning the extension of mourning, and yet that usage brings us back to a related question: what meaning are we to ascribe to the fact that the limits to which the injunction of mourning exposes us are not only those of an *I*, but those of a *we*? What collectivity, what community, are we talking about?

Once the anticipation of mourning or of memory, both impossible and necessary, are confided to a *we,* inquiry turns to the obstacles, limitations, and restrictions that are imposed on that duty's universalization. By what right can some or other *we* contend that, outside the limits of some determinate circle (friends, family fellow citizens, religion, or some other form of fraternity), death, before it happens, is already and forever a matter of indifference—that there shall be neither mourning nor memory *of the others*? And yet, as surely as we share the memory of wars, deportations, genocides, organized or tolerated famine, terror, and all the anonymous deaths in mass graves and on the killing fields, we know that there is no injustice, no violence, that is not accompanied by the claim to just such a right. We also know that the relation to the death of others is exclusive, that the dead "are not all equal" [*n'ont pas le même prix*], that we do not bestow the same importance on the death of some as we do on that of others—and that the apportionments that are at stake in this bestowing or withholding of value are forbidding. Such is the meaning of our finitude: the delimitation of the I through the experience of the other, as mortal, is contingent on a regime of experience that is always one of deletion [*l'exception*]—the deletion of an experience of the other, and thus others, such that, for some among them, the possibility that they might die and shall have to be mourned, and their memory preserved, does not (or does no longer) enter into consideration. Violence and injustice, in other words, always suppose that *the welcome,* that *hospitality*—which, in the relation to the other, makes the anticipation of mourning and memory possible—are suspended, and even eclipsed.

Thus we are drawn back to the path down which we started, the path traced by the conjunction between two "definitions" or "circumscriptions" of ethics, one which ties ethics to mourning, and one which ties it to hospitality. In the work of Derrida, as in the constellation of writings that he so singularly inspired, there is one dialogue— a dialogue that is at the same time an homage to a departed friend— that exhibits this ethics in an exemplary way. I speak, of course, of his *Adieu to Emmanuel Levinas,* Derrida's engagement with the thought of Levinas which he undertook the year following Levinas's death. If we turn to this dialogue now, it is not simply because it thematizes what the thinking of one author owes to that of the other, but because it works through, decisively, the question of the extension of the responsibility of mourning and remembrance beyond the limits of friendship. It is plainly a text of farewell. Like so many others, it is a text that takes up and bears responsibility for the thought, the words, and the phrases of a friend who has been silenced. But the word that retains this friend's attention, the word in which the piety of mourning and remembrance is concentrated, is the word "welcome": a welcome extended to the face of the other, the face that signifies first and foremost the other's vulnerability and mortality.

We saw earlier that the possibility of mourning elicits an impossible *affirmation.* Hence the question of mourning's limits turns on whether this affirmation is somehow conditioned or conditional—and, if this is the case, what is doing the conditioning, whether some or other attachment, or a belonging, or a shared history. Common sense tells us, it goes without saying, that this affirmation should have limits, that we should not have to shoulder the burden of mourning just any other. On the contrary, we should be able to make distinctions. And yet a hyperbolic ethics [*l'éthique hyperbolique*], in its radicality, enjoins us to think otherwise. Mourning, because it is "ethics itself," cannot be restricted. How, then, are we to understand, according to this train of thought, the universal character of the affirmation that is being made? The hypothesis that we shall consider here is that, for Derrida, this affirmation echoes the *double yes* that he learned from Levinas, the yes *of* the other and the yes *to* the other, wherein are concentrated, there where they are indissociable, attention to the speech of the other, and the welcome of his face, or hospitality: "And since it opens itself to the infinity of the other, an infinity that, as other, in some sense precedes it, the welcoming *of* the other (objective genitive), will already be a response: the *yes to* the other will already be responding to the welcoming *of* the other (subjective genitive), to the *yes* of the other. This response is called for *as soon as* the infinite—always *of* the other—is welcomed."[7]

The responsibility of mourning and memory is one of a response that precedes supplication. Responsibility means that we are always *tributary* to that which we promise to the other, even before he has appealed to us. This is the very meaning of our finitude. "Ethics itself" is *both mourning and hospitality,* not only because it enjoins us to *anticipate* the appeal of the other, to welcome the other even before we are asked, but because what we welcome in the other [*accueillons de lui*] is indissociable from his *mortality*—that is, from the possibility of our having to mourn him one day and keep him in our memory. Derrida does not connect or superimpose either of these two "definitions" of ethics unambiguously, nor does he explicitly associate the theme of *originary mourning* with that of *unconditional hospitality*. Rather, they are the subject of numerous but separate developments. But if one reads attentively the texts that he devotes to each of these themes independently, one encounters the same terms being used to think through both the one and the other. Thus, in his reading of Levinas, he maintains that the welcome, *like mourning,* is of necessity "to *receive* [Levinas's emphasis] from the Other beyond the capacity of the I, which means exactly: to have the idea of infinity."[8]

If it is true then, as he states in *Memoirs for Paul de Man,* that the I does not appear to itself otherwise than as the trace of the other in us, and that this trace always supposes a memory in mourning—and that, consequently, "everything that we inscribe in the living present of our relation to others already carries, always, the signature of *memoirs-from-beyond-the-grave*"[9]—if all this is true, then we must locate the reason for it in our hospitality, which is nothing other than our disposedness toward welcoming, in the encounter with the face, the *vulnerability* and the *mortality* of the other. We know that this welcome precedes all knowledge, all identification, all characterization. It cannot be contained by knowledge, by any practical consideration, and it is not subject to any condition of belonging. It does not allow for compromise [*repli*] or restriction. Inversely, if some regime of exception is imposed on welcoming, the discrimination inherent in its apportionment always carries with it the implication of violence and injustice. Hence the mortality of the other exceeds the capacity of the I in two ways. First, it overflows this capacity *singularly*. Just as the anticipation of mourning and memory is both impossible and necessary, because it cannot claim to achieve the ideal and integral interiorization of the other, so does the welcome of the face mean exposing oneself to the transcendence of its radical separateness, which exceeds this same capacity in essence. Second, it overflows this capacity *by its universal extension*. We asked above how it is possible for the *precession* [*devancement*] *of mourning* not to be limited to friends and those close to us. The answer is in the "unconditional hospitality" that is granted to the face of any and every other as mortal. There is doubtless nothing more difficult to imagine and think through. The universality of mourning encounters the same resistance as hospitality. To anticipate mourning and the memory of any and every other, and to welcome the mortality that is exposed in the face, seem to require a measure of responsibility that is impossible if not excessive. But ethics, Derrida tells us, cannot be thought of otherwise. It is because mourning and hospitality share this hyperbolical characteristic that they are "ethics itself."

The fact remains, as we bear in mind the violence and injustice of forgetting or negating the twofold responsibility (the two-dimensional face [*double face*] of ethics) implied by the mortality of the other, and as we recall, as did, by turn, Levinas and Derrida, that we cannot speak of hospitality, memory, and mourning without being mindful of all the denials of hospitality, of all the abandonments, all the violent deaths, the deportations, and the extermination of millions upon millions of individuals that mark the last century—without, that is to say, evoking and invoking history alongside the present. The responsibility that we must think through is not simply an ethical one. It becomes political. Specifically, our attention is directed to the *passage* from the one to the other, from ethics to politics. In *Adieu to Emmanuel Levinas,* where Derrida works his way through *Totality and Infinity, Otherwise Than Being, Beyond Essence,* and some of the Talmudic readings, he registers his concern precisely with this passage by assigning importance to Levinas's political texts—that is, to texts that grapple with issues of contemporary significance, such as the *Cities of Refuge* or "Politics After!" (in *Beyond the Verse: Talmudic Readings and Lectures*). He is preoccupied by the need ultimately to tackle one of the "political questions" that, along with apartheid and the death penalty, trouble him the most: the future of Israel, of Jerusalem, and the Israeli–Palestinian conflict.

In this perspective, he quotes a long passage from Levinas's "Peace and Proximity":

> Doubtless, responsibility for the other human being is, in its *immediacy, anterior to every question*. But how does responsibility obligate if a third troubles this exteriority of two where my subjection of the subject is subjection to the neighbor? The third is other than the neighbor but also another neighbor, and also a neighbor of the other, and not simply their fellow. What am I to do? What have they already done to one another? Who passes before the other in my responsibility? What, then, are the other and the third with respect to one another? *Birth of the question.*[10]

What could this passage (between ethics and politics) be? What is meant by politics coming after (according to the title of Levinas's article)? In what way do the anticipation of mourning and memory, as explored by Derrida in *Memoirs for Paul de Man,* and the hospitality for mortality, which he adopts from Levinas, come before? As Derrida endeavors to address these questions, he is drawn to a word (it is difficult to determine whether we are dealing here with an idea, a notion, or a concept) whose decisive importance he promptly acknowledges: the word *peace*. In effect, what is in play in our assessment of the articulation between ethics and politics—and particularly in the way that we tie them to questions of mourning, memory, mortality, and hospitality—is nothing less than our understanding of peace, of peace among human beings, without regard for affiliations, all claims to identity, and thus our understanding of "fraternity" and of "humanity," having been suspended. *Hospitality, humanity, fraternity*: Derrida, in his examination of Levinas's "The Nations and the Presence of Israel,"[11] does not recoil from pointing out the equivalence of these three concepts, despite the fact that two of them at least, humanity and fraternity, were among those whose deconstruction revealed an infinitely problematic, even aporetic character.

What does the twofold, hyperbolical exigency [*exigence*] of ethics (the exigency of the anticipation of mourning and that of hospitality) mean? First and foremost, it means that peace is first [*première*]—that humanity cannot be conceptualized independently of a structuring relation to the vulnerability and mortality of the other, to his welcoming (and to the anticipation of mourning that welcoming calls for). Peace does not come *afterward* to compensate or correct some original hostility that would define the "natural" relationship between human beings, as in Kant's *Toward Perpetual Peace*.[12] For Derrida, the work of Levinas is crucial on this point (even though Derrida, at this same point, will detach his thinking from that of Levinas as we will see below). It is not enough to say that the self only appears to itself as the trace of the other and that it is always in mourning. It is also necessary to affirm that this trace is not a bearer of war, that it is not marked by the seal of a primal [*première*] hostility. It all comes down to the irreducibility of peace to some politics in which it could be confined—it all comes down to the way that an ethics of mourning and hospitality ("ethics itself") invalidates and rejects all invocations of ancient hatreds, of incompatible affiliations, whether religious, national, or other, or of some clash or shock of peoples, nations, races, or civilizations—of history itself and collective memory—to suspend and even eclipse the command of ethics. Nothing—not geopolitical, economic, or industrial calculations, not some alliance and the compromises that enable it—authorizes a "we," a determinate community, to stand on such an invocation (and in so doing, lay the ground for a culture of fear and the cultivation of an enemy) in order to spurn this twofold ethics:[13] "What is peace? What are we saying when we say 'peace'? What does it mean 'to be at peace with'—to be at peace with someone else, a group, a State, a nation, oneself as another? In each of these cases, one can be at peace only with some other. So long as what is other as other will not have been in some way 'welcomed' in epiphany, in the withdrawal or visitation of its face, it would make no sense to speak of peace."[14]

Two tasks are then compulsory. The first is to understand, each time singularly, if and how politics on behalf of the third, which remains necessary, perverts or respects ethics. There is no doubt that one cannot decide, regulate, or establish norms in advance (Derrida reminds us of this constantly). But we know—as surely as we remain the powerless witnesses of so many crimes committed in the name of some conditional right that some set of persons has granted to itself (which we will call here the twofold denial of hospitality and mortality), and as surely as we know that the twofold exigency of ethics is everywhere overlooked—that there is no limit to the denial of ethics, and therefore no limit to violence and injustice. Thus it happens that such or some or other category (or some or other grouping of individuals) can be abandoned to the most extreme misery, destitution, or insecurity, reduced to famine, stigmatized and persecuted, imprisoned, detained, expelled, deported, and even exterminated. Hence the second task: to hear the distress of those whose mortality is no longer perceived or acknowledged and to come to their aid by *deducing* a politics from ethics.[15]

What might this politics be, if mourning and hospitality are "ethics itself"? Derrida reminds us that Levinas never answers this question explicitly. His silence, however, has the force of an injunction, and even a command. If it is true that ethics must be conceptualized as the welcome reserved for the transcendence of the other—a welcome that will always signify what Derrida termed unconditional hospitality—and if it is true that this hospitality has its foundation in the mortality of the other, then *it is this mortality that politics can never disregard*. Politics must never forget, in any engagement, in any decision, that it is the singular relation to mortality and vulnerability that matters, and that enables us to discern and differentiate what must necessarily be apportioned [*faire la part des unes et des autres*]—and that all discourse, all argumentation, all propaganda, but also all theories and all philosophies that pretend to disregard this relation, are missing the essential:

> It seems to dictate this to me: the *formal* injunction of the deduction remains irrecusable, and it does not wait any more than the third and justice do. Ethics enjoins a politics and a law: this dependence and the direction of this conditional derivation are as irreversible as they are unconditional. But the political or juridical *content* that is thus assigned remains undetermined, still to be determined beyond knowledge, beyond all presentation, all concepts, all possible intuition, in a singular way, in the speech and the responsibility *taken* by each person, in each situation, and on the basis of an analysis that is each time unique—unique and infinite, unique but *a priori* exposed to substitution, unique and yet general, interminable in spite of the urgency of the decision.[16]

But what exactly does politics [*elle*] forget, or *eclipse*? How and where do injustice and violence begin? In the passage quoted above, there is at least one statement that can point us down a decisive path. It is the insistence with which Jacques Derrida says again and again that a responsible analysis is "each time unique"—that is, an analysis that subjects the political decision to the ethical injunction of anticipated mourning, memory, and hospitality—assuming, reading the texts together, that these three *responses* could ever be separated. This evocation of *uniqueness* [*l'unicité*] echoes in effect Derrida's use of this same concept in *The Work of Mourning*[17] and in "Rams: Uninterrupted Dialogue," to call to mind what is signified by each and every disappearance: the end of the world, in totality. The uniqueness of the other,[18] inappropriable and irreplaceable, irreducible to knowledge and to assimilation, is the concern of ethics. Once ethics is exposed to the other's mortality, each time singularly, once it anticipates the mourning of the other and welcomes its vulnerability, *before any mediation*, it can no longer recognize a common or collective identity, or allow itself to generalize, to globalize, or even to classify or to characterize. But politics, in contrast, must rely on just such determinations. Its strategies, calculations, interests, and reasoning plunge it into this form of generalization, of which the compiling of statistics is merely one facet among others. There is no state, no government, or even institution that does not indulge in accounting, numbering and quantifying—and we know, as surely as we remember the wars of the last century, how lethal can be the will to alter those numbers, to control them, to bend reality to the idea, whether ideal or phantasm, that they imply. When this will falls prey to madness, we also know that neither the mortality nor the vulnerability of singular individuals, as they summon each of us to responsibility, can resist it—and so the singularity and uniqueness of lives is lost and their memory even erased: "The political dissimulates because it brings to light. It hides what it throws light on. Giving the face to be seen, bringing or attracting it into the space of public phenomenality, it thereby renders it invisible. Visibility renders invisible its invisibility, that is, the withdrawal of its epiphany. But exhibiting the invisibility of the face is not the only way of dissimulating it. The violence of the political mistreats the face yet again by effacing its unicity in a generality."[19]

If politics can be deduced from ethics, that deduction depends, first and foremost, on a radical transformation in our relation to the mortality of the other. Death cannot be thought, calculated, or accepted (assuming it has not been decided or even caused), in the ignorance of what death means each time singularly. Death, in other words, cannot be reduced to an element in some or other computation. "The epiphany of the face" cannot be sacrificed on the altar of interests. Derrida retains from his reading of Levinas the thought of this "'concept,' peace, . . . [that] would go beyond any thought that

would wish to remain *purely* political."[20] This overflow, the flow of
ethics *into* and *over* [*sur et dans*] politics, reminds us that any peace
that turns its back on the mortality and vulnerability of the (determinate or indeterminate) other, because of some or other "allergy," that
any peace that would accept a compromise regarding the retention
or confinement of the other in misery and insecurity, or that would
resign itself to abandoning the other, or that would accommodate itself
to the death of the other, whether probable, certain, or programmed,
is not peace.[21]

Linking together two "definitions" of ethics (ethics as hospitality and
ethics as mourning), as we have done here from the outset, is not
merely a debt, an inspiration, or an incitement and convergence that
becomes suddenly apparent. It is also a decisive digression, divergence,
and departure [*écart*]. For if Derrida can conceive of mourning as
"ethics itself," he can only do so against the backdrop of that "originary mourning" that, to his knowledge, as he states in *Aporias,* neither Heidegger, nor Freud, nor Levinas took into account.[22] As we
saw above, Levinas, in his protracted confrontation with Heidegger's
thought on Being-toward-death, affirms again and again that the death
of the other is the first death, in opposition to the privilege that Heidegger accords to the mineness of dying. In doing so, he affirms my
responsibility for the other *as mortal.* Derrida does not question this
responsibility. Indeed it traverses all his thinking on hospitality. What
he is contesting, on the contrary, is the irreducible and painful opposition—to which the memory of war is not foreign—between *my*
death and the death of the other. And in doing so he grounds his dis-
sent in his conceptualization of originary mourning as a way to think
about "surviving."

Another dialogue thus comes into play—as if, in Derrida's reading
of Levinas a third name had to be made to resonate and to reinforce

the constellation. This third name is that of Maurice Blanchot. There is nothing in the thought of death and the memory of war that is more striking than the echoes produced by the intersections and mutual references between the works of Levinas, Blanchot, and Derrida (to which one should also add the writings of Paul Celan). The investigation in which they partake mutually, reading and writing in the problematic shadow of Heidegger's analyses, is literally haunted by the memory of war.

The whole question then is to understand how the recognition of an originary mourning comes to modify the rigorous partition between the relation of each and everyone to his own death and the relation of each and everyone to the death of the other. Derrida, in *Aporias,* poses the problem in these terms:

> If *Jemeinigkeit,* that of *Dasein* or that of the ego (in the common sense, the psychoanalytic sense, or Levinas's sense) is constituted in its ipseity in terms of an originary mourning, then this self-relation welcomes or supposes the other within its being-itself as different from itself. And reciprocally: the relation to the other (in itself outside myself, outside myself in myself) will never be distinguishable from a bereaved apprehension. The relevance of this question of knowing whether it is from one's own proper death or from the other's death that the relation to death or the certitude of death is instituted is thus limited from the start.[23]

In other words, the relation that each of us maintains with his or her own death, and the relation that each of us maintains with the death of the other who renders us originarily responsible for the mortality of all others, are indissociable. They are inextricably mingled. No one anticipates his own death without also anticipating at the same time the death of the other. Once there is no self, no relation to self without the experience of mourning and the onus of memory, without the anticipation of both mourning and remembering together, then the death of each and everyone bears, first and foremost, the death of the other in us. It bears that death all the more since mourning is always destined to fail, as shown by Derrida's critical interrogation of Abraham and Torok's opposition between incorporation and intro-jection in their discussion of Freud.[24] No matter what I do, no matter what anyone does, neither I nor the other will be able to "incorpo-rate, interiorize, introject, subjectivize the other in me."[25] If it is true that the relation to one's mortality is constitutive of the self, then the self cannot be supervised, normalized, or regulated once and for all. On the contrary, it is the self's unfinished character, its visitation, its haunting that make the self what it is—that make *me* what *I am*. This law Derrida calls the *cogito of mourning*: "Even before the death of the other, the inscription in me of her or his mortality constitutes me. I mourn therefore I am, I am—dead with the death of the other, my relation to myself is first of all plunged into mourning, a mourning that is moreover impossible."[26]

We can thus better understand the impressive complexity of Der-rida's reading of Levinas's thought on death. It all comes down to the complementarity of the *hospitality* conferred on the mortality of the other (as thematized by Levinas) and of its inscription in the form of an impossible *mourning*. On the one hand, Derrida inherits from Lev-inas the question of hospitality, understood as a welcoming of the transcendence of the other; on the other hand, he displaces that wel-coming by giving this receptivity the dimension of a constitutive mourning [*endeuillement*]. Ethics therefore cannot be rigorously the same [*même*]. The "I" no longer has to sacrifice the relation that it has to its own death (the mineness of dying) for the sake of its responsibil-ity for the death of the other since this mineness, to the extent that it is always already in mourning, does not exist outside of this respon-sibility.[27] This displacement, moreover, is indissociably linked to a con-cept—that of *survivance*—to which Derrida assigns the importance of a "universal structure." The claim that mourning is originary means in effect that "death has already occurred," that its very imminence—as that which is to come and which I fear—already belongs to the past, but to a past that has never been present.[28] What is ineluctable is not so much that death will come one day, but rather the fact that it has already come. This is the lesson that Derrida retains from his reading of Maurice Blanchot's *The Instant of My Death* and *The Writing of Disaster*: "Death has already arrived, because it is inescapable. One is not resuscitated from this experience of inescapable death, even if one survives it. One can only survive it without surviving it."[29]

What constitutes the self is not the relation that each of us maintains toward one's own death, as one's ownmost possibility, nor the relation we maintain with the death of the other, as the death for which we assume responsibility. What constitutes the self is what Derrida, following Blanchot, calls "the encounter of death with death"—its relentless imminence and its immemorial past. Though living, I have already died a thousand deaths, each one indissociably both mine and that of the other whom I endeavor to survive. The richness of Derrida's analyses cannot be fully replicated here. But the displacement that he effects elicits at least two concluding remarks. First, though Blanchot's account relates a singular narrative, this singularity is nevertheless "universalizable."[30] It bears within it a universality that is less directly that of death or life, of the fear of death or the attachment to life, than one of a sharing of a *survivance* that overflows their opposition. All living beings live and die of their survival [*vit et meurt de sa survie*] between two deaths, "in the moratorium of an encounter of the death outside of him with the death that is already dying in him."[31] The second remark follows from the first. If this *survivance* is the affliction [*passion*] of a difference—the affliction of immortality as death—then it is this affliction that ultimately gives meaning to the expression "we mortals":

And what he knows, what he imagines is that one death runs *after* the other: runs down, pursues and chases, hunts the other. From the moment it chases the other, pursues the other in order to catch up with it, one can hypothesize that it pushes away and excludes the death that it chases in this way, that it also protects itself in the passion of this *permanent differance* [*différance à demeure*], of this *undying as differance* [*demourance comme différance*]. What remains for him of existence, more than this race to death, is this race of death in view of death *in order* not to see death coming.[32]

We tried earlier to understand how ethics and politics, conjointly with mourning and hospitality, could acquire a universal dimension. Ultimately they all stand on their shared injunction of this *differance*. Far from presuming some or other complacency toward death, they are, in the final analysis, an affirmation of life, as a sharing in mortality, which overflows the attachment of each of us to our own life. The affliction of survivance (of undying as *differance*) is therefore necessarily ("this is ethics itself") a *compassion*.

8

The Thought of Death and the Image of the Dead

We live day in and day out with images of death. They are foisted on us at regular hours of the day. We encounter them at newsstands, both in magazines and in the publicity for magazines. They continually invade the televised news. They participate in the coverage of events whose distinctive character, whose primary character is to *convey death* [*mortifère*], to present, that is, to present *us with* (to bring to us) images of death. Whether they be images of war, of assassinations, of natural catastrophes, spectacular accidents, death *makes* news [*actualité*].[1] What is given to us *as* news (*as* the event of the day, day after day) consists of a certain presentation of death—of a death that is always *violent*, whose victims are many, and which interrupts, brutally and unforeseeably, lives that are always anonymous. For it must be said that, of the great number of dead who *make* the news—victims of catastrophes, accidents, wars, assassinations, or random attacks—we do not (and never will) know their names.

But, in a form that is *apparently* different, we also encounter images in works of fiction, whether through television or the cinema (not to mention video games), that describe in their own way *another* actuality, that of an entertainment, that is no less a *conveyor of death* and is no less imposed on us than the actuality of news programs, despite the fact that they seek to provide distraction from that actuality. But the difference is only *apparent*, for the boundary that separates one "culture of death" from the other is unclear. The effects of the one on the other are difficult to discern, whether we try to measure the impact of fiction on the (scenographic or dramaturgical) presentation of the news, or, inversely, the implication of "news," marked by violent death, on the creation of these same works of fiction—of fiction that provides death with another reality. When we say, moreover, that "reality" surpasses fiction or that fiction "anticipates [*devance*] reality," we are referring to the possibility of just such an indiscernibility, as well as to what that indiscernibility owes to the images of death, around which both reality and fiction are constructed, and, not without calculation, are intermixed.

What is the meaning of the fact that *we* live in common [*communément*] with such images? Three kinds of question are suggested by this fact, prior to any consideration of ethics (whether in its defense or its castigation), prior to any sociological or psychological analysis, prior to any calculation of their effects (whether compassion, indignation, or revolt). The first concerns the meaning to be given to the expression "to make the news" [*faire l'actualité*]. Does it mean, as regards death, that there is nothing more "newsworthy" [*actuel*] than death's various manifestations, understood as so many effects of a *disordered* [*déréglé*] relationship between human beings, between human beings and the world, or between human beings and the planet? Or does it mean that *news* is made (fabricated, constructed, organized, and sometimes even "fictionalized") from death's image? And if this is the case, what is the motivation, what are the stakes involved, in focusing that construction on such images? The second kind of question interrogates the collective destination of these images. They are in effect never addressed to a singular individual. To the extent that they are imposed on "us," on us all at the same time, and to the extent that they occupy the same public space, they participate in the constitution of a collective subject. We live *with* these images, but we also live *with* others, *with* whom we receive these images passively, without really sharing them, even if, in the best case, we resent them now and then, even if we demonstrate our uneasiness about having to put up with them day after day, and, less frequently, even if we analyze them and comment on them. Regarding the images of death, we must ask ourselves what they make of "us"—that is to say, what is the "us" that they are making?[2] We will see below that this question is eminently political—that related to images and representations of death (and to the history and technology of their production) are questions of community and belonging, and occasionally of the lethal identitarian digressions that they enable. This is no doubt true of all presentations of the news. We have only to recall the exhorbitant privilege that the news accords to the "national," the "local," or the "regional" to appreciate its readiness to expand its horizons in order to focus on events that occur, under the sign of death, elsewhere.[3] When the "news" takes an interest in the rest of the world, it does so in order to present images of death—as if such images constituted the only possible way to *open* up to the rest of the world the "we" to whom they are addressed. But when we ask what is it that we share [*partageons*] (or do not share) with and in such images, a third, more arduous kind of question arises. What is the relationship between this sharing or non-sharing and the thought of death? Do these presentations or representations (the terms invite analysis) *make us* think of death? Or should we not say, in a gesture toward Pascal, that they turn us away, distract us, or "divert" us from thinking about death? Is it the common thought of death or is it the common absence of thought that brings us together (even though this "us" remains undetermined)? Or if the thought of death can be shared in a way that cannot be reduced to the sharing of such images, what is the *other* "us" that is being *otherwise* constituted?

These three questions do not belong exclusively to our time. Neither the question of the (political or religious) exploitation of the images of death, nor their collective sharing, nor their complex relation to the thought of death was foreign to the late Middle Ages, for example, as the "Black Death" ravaged Europe's cities and countrysides. Ingmar Bergman's *The Seventh Seal*, several scenes of which address the questions asked here, has much to teach us about the images of death. Relevant to the first question is a scene in which a troop of actors, which will later place itself under the protection of the knight Antonius Block, is discussing the play that they will stage for the feast of All Saints, and the representation of death that was commissioned [*commandée*] (in every sense of the term) by the religious authorities. "The priests," says the director of the troop (who will be the first to be claimed by death), "are speculating about violent death." Squire Jöns, a little later, asks the painter about the dance of death to which he is giving the final touch, to which the latter replies by invoking the authorities' need to terrorize the people. Relevant to the second question is a later scene in which a preacher of death (in the Nietzschean sense of the term) is haranguing the crowd, reminding everyone of their pending demise ("Know, fools, that you are going to die"). Squire Jöns, again, displays a critical stance regarding the imagery of the preacher's oration, lampooning what he calls "the jargon of death." Finally, it is obviously the game of chess, opposing the knight and the personification of death (the image par excellence of death—the image of all the images and of all the death masks), that relates to the third question and will carry the interrogation of this imagery to its culminating point. When the knight, recently returned from the Crusades, asks what is the meaning of death, the figure of death replies that it, itself, does not have the slightest idea. The dark silhouette who personifies death, who personifies all the images of death, like a living mask, declares that it has (and will forever have) *nothing* to teach us.

Hence the question that should orient our interrogation: What is this thought of death, as thought that is *common* to us all and is *shared* in our encounter with the images of death, as our lot and our common fate? The paradox of this thought is this: nothing envelops us in solitude more effectively than this encounter. The relationship that each of us maintains with her own finitude (and with that of others), anticipating in thought the time of her disappearance (or that of those near to her), is singular.[4] It is indeed this relationship that makes the absolute singularity of each of us, in the sense that no one other than me can think in my place about my own disappearance, or can think like me (in the same terms) of the disappearance of people near to me. We have trouble speaking about such thoughts, about the anxiety that seizes us when we can no longer escape them, when we can no longer escape the vertigo into which they transport us. And yet we hold nothing more in common than such thoughts. Thoughts of death (our own, and that of others, near to us, less near to us, relations and friends) traverse all cultures and transcend all belonging. There is nothing that we can know more assuredly about one another than *the fact* of such thoughts, no matter how they might vary. *We* think about death, we know that others (*all others*) think about it, we know that *we* think about it—and yet such thoughts are not constitutive of a "we." They do not *bring us together*. Bossuet, Pascal, and even Nietzsche[5] all said it: what we have most in common is what we share the least—not even with those who are closest to us.[6]

To say that such "sharing" is nevertheless possible always elicits surprise and astonishment. If we are to believe Plato's *Phaedo,* this was certainly the case for Simmias and Cebes, Socrates's interlocutors in this most extraordinary dialogue. *Phaedo* is not merely a philosophical text on death (perhaps the first and most celebrated of all such texts, inspiring commentary throughout the history of Western philosophy), and thus of thought on death (of thought on death among other kinds of thought, and at the origin of so much thinking), but a meditation on the sharing of such thought. It is the very possibility of such sharing, rather than postponement, tears, terror, or dread, that is in question—a possibility that is improbable to the point that it surprises the dialogue's interlocutors, over and over again, whenever they experience it.

The scene, which Phaedo relates to Echecrates, is the following: Phaedo, in the company of Simmias, Cebes, and others, has come to visit Socrates in prison and provide him with support and encouragement in the final moments before his execution. Here they are, then, reunited with their teacher. But they are immediately put off balance by his lack of affliction and apprehension. No despondency, no dread, no anguish are apparent either in his gestures or in his words. Socrates seems to belie all the representations of death that portray it as something terrifying. Those who have come to be with him and to support him (and perhaps even to console him) find that their roles are reversed. For Socrates to be so detached, he must be possessed of a *thought of death* so robust as to challenge conventional imagery— a thought that they immediately ask him to *share*: "'Well,' said Simmias, 'do you intend to go away, Socrates, and keep your opinion to yourself, or would you *let us share it*? It seems to me that this is a good which belongs in common to us also.'"[7]

What is given, as death is imminent, in the ultimate anticipation of death, is the sharing of a thought, whose explication and discussion will consume the entire—or rather, *almost* the entire—dialogue. *Almost*, because the dialogue will conclude with a narration (perhaps an image) that prolongs or continues this thought. Here, in Socrates's words, is the thought: "Well, then, this is what we call *death*, is it not, a release and separation of the soul from the body?"[8]

But this release is not only what we call death. It is also what we call thought. In effect, thinking for Plato assumes that the soul is no longer wholly taken up by the needs of the body, and that it detaches itself, releases itself, frees itself from the body (its sensations, its pleasures, and also no doubt its raptures [*délire*]). The result is a community of essence between death and thought. This community of essence sheds light on the scene of the dialogue. The imminence of death becomes thought's own time (at least for the wise), since the soul, in all its life, has never been so close to its liberation. And thought is never closer to apprehending itself than when, freed from its dread and apprehension, it thinks about death. Both thought and death attain to their essence, the one through the other. Thought apprehends itself by being thought of death, and death allows itself to become known when, by overcoming what we fear to lose in death (all that *attaches* us to life), we make it the object of our thought.

But that which attaches and binds us (including to one another) is also that which we imagine having as our own (beginning with our body). The attachment [*liaison*] (unlike the release) extends to all the spheres of mineness [*du propre*] and appropriation (face and shape, goods, honors). That is why thought (including the thought of death) is not really thought unless it is at the same time *disappropriation*. Inversely, the fear of death (or the refusal to think about it) reveals our attachment to these same figures of mineness [*propre*]. We fear death *to the extent* that we *hold on* [*tenons*] to what we are and to what we possess [*détenons*]: "'Then is it not,' said Socrates, 'a sufficient indication, when you see a man troubled because he is going to die, that he was not a lover of wisdom but a lover of the body? And this same man is also a lover of money and of honor, one or both?'"[9]

What do *we* hold on to? What is it that holds *us* [*tient*] and holds *us* back [*maintient*]? This is undoubtedly the principle question of the dialogue. The imminence of death (of my own, as of that of the other), its ultimate anticipation, its ultimate advance, provide a propitious time to think about what *holds* us. Of essential importance here is that this question is one that is *shared*. If thought assumes, like the death that it anticipates (and in keeping with its image), the release of figures of mineness, it is implied that this sharing is also (and perhaps above all) one of *disappropriation* [*désappropriation*]. To these friends who wonder what they can share with Socrates in the last minutes granted to him, Socrates responds, "To look otherwise on what holds *us* and what *we* hold on to."

This *other* look [*regard*] is *other* only by its difference from the look that directs our attention to the things that we love (that we say we *hold dear* [*tenir*]): our bodies, our goods, our honors. We note in passing (we will return to this) that Socrates does not mention family and friends—he does not, at any time during the dialogue, evoke death as a separation from family and friends, or the imminence of death as the anticipation of mourning, or the release of death as an ordeal for the survivors of the deceased. Never does he envisage death, except furtively, by avoiding the question, from the point of view of those whom I (you, he, she) *hold dear* and by whom I (you, he, she) am held dear. Such is the paradox of the *Phaedo*. The *sharing of thought* is lacking the basic meaning [*sens premier*] of death, which is, specifically, death as the interruption of the dialogue that enables this sharing, thus rendering it impossible.[10] And yet the words exchanged by Socrates and his companions (and staged by Plato) have no meaning [*sens*] other than to enact this other look on death (and on life), as a *shared look*.

But there is another feature that makes for the *alterity* of this dialogue—a feature that is revealed by asking what thought *consists* of. Plato devotes the most important part of the dialogue to this question. Thought is *other* because it is fundamentally *reminiscence*. To think is to remember what one has learned. The anticipation of death (even as it is imminent) is a propitious time for remembering knowledge that has become buried [*enfoui*]. And as it so happens, what we remember, at this precise moment—what Socrates is *sharing* with his friends—is the reminiscence of death itself, of what is meant by each death singularly; that is, the recollection of what life holds not in a general way, but of what *a* life holds, each life in its singularity.

A widespread belief invokes something of this reminiscence in the case of the person who, having faced peril and believing his time has come, recalls reliving his life as if fast-forwarded in a film. In such circumstances the anticipation of the release that is death is conjugated in the future anterior: "This is what my life shall have been, this is what I shall have done."

One must nevertheless introduce a qualification. If the anticipation of death (as thought or apprehension) implies remembrance, the object of remembrance is not necessarily thought. It all depends, Socrates explains, on the way we have lived—on the things our life was attached to. If it was marked by what Socrates calls "the human ills" (which he enumerates as "error and folly and fear and fierce loves"), the only possible memory will be fear itself.[11] Thought will be marred by this fear—which is first of all the fear of losing that with which, and thanks to which, I do everything possible to escape thought, notably the thought of death. These ills, as we know, are a function of our attachment to our bodies—of the bond that we will have sustained with that "which one can touch and see and drink and eat and employ in the pleasures of love."[12] The remembrance of such things, if we follow Plato, is what blocks out any thought of release. Inversely, if one's life is marked by the exercise of such thinking (what Socrates calls "the life of the philosopher")—which is to say by the apprenticeship of release—it is this memory that will prevail at the time of death. Hence the idea inscribed at the core of Plato's dialogue, the inheritance of which is assumed by the whole history of Western thought, "Thinking is nothing other than the preparation for death": "If [the soul] departs pure, dragging with it nothing of the body, because it never willingly associated with the body in life, but avoided it and gathered itself into itself alone, since this has always been its constant study—but this means nothing else than that it pursued philosophy rightly and really practiced being in a state of death: or is not this the practice of death?"[13]

With this thought (thought as preparation for death) I suspend this long but necessary (and yet incomplete) detour through Plato's *Phaedo,* and advance three conclusions that bring us back to the problem of the imagery of death. First, though Plato's argument rests on a pre-supposed stigmatization of the body that we, like Nietzsche, can suspect conceals *ressentiment* toward life, it nevertheless prods us to meditate on the bond that ties all thought of death to the affects (or ideally, for Plato, the absence of affects) of the body. Unless we conform ourselves to Plato's image of the philosopher (the model of which, even for his friends, is Socrates), we think of death with a body that has always already been touched by death—and that retains its memory. We *live,* sometimes unaware, *with* the memory of these affects. Our thoughts wrestle with this memory, of which the origin, the constitution, the successive strata are the most unfathomable part of our existence. From this observation emerge an endless number of questions. Can, and should, this memory be "educated"? Assuming that it is simultaneously individual and collective (that it therefore always incorporates the dimension of a sharing), how does it determine or affect the relations that attach *us* to one another? What does this *us* designate? How far does the sharing of this memory extend? What fractures, what frontiers (cultural, political, or even economic) does it inscribe?

All these questions mean that, in seeking to examine the "images of death," as we are ultimately doing, it is this *memory* that comes into question. This leads us to a second remark. There are obviously other images of death than those that have attracted our attention up to this point—other images that occupy our shared memory. Besides the imagery of music and poetry, each "visitation" of Christian visual art, for example, exposes us to such images. And this of course applies more generally to all Western visual art. Some of these images evoke the horrors of war, like the etchings of Jacques Callot, *Les Misères et Malheurs de la Guerre* (1633), or those of Goya, *Los desastres de la guerra,* produced between 1810 and 1820[14]—or again the drawings of Otto Dix and George Grosz. But other artists depict a very different thought of death, as, for example, the various representations of *Vanitas* by Pieter Claesz, Pieter Boel, David Bailly, or Antonio de Pereda, all of which recall our common end by depicting a human skull among various objects such as coins, jewels, weapons, books, or musical scores.[15] What criterion do we invoke to make distinctions between these various *images*? Realism, imagination, artistry? Among the criteria we might muster, it is memory that I shall adopt here as a common thread. Simply put, the sixteenth- and seventeenth-century portrayals of *Vanitas,* the engravings of Callot and Goya, are not *consigned to memory* in the same way as the fictions of cinema or television or, even less so, the images of newspapers and magazines. It is not simply because the substance and animation of these media differ (the canvas, the cinema screen, the computer screen, the paper of the photograph or the news journal). It is rather because these images are not constituted (cut, detached, or assembled in series, framed or mounted) with the same expectation. How they are constituted depends on their target audience and the way they address that audience. News, like fiction (cinematographic or televisual)— films of war and films of catastrophes—are formatted and mounted so as to reach the broadest possible audience. The images of death that they present are intended to hold the attention (and, by the *power* of repetition, to be inscribed *by force* in the memory) of the largest number. In the last resort, the obsession with audience (as figure of the universal) prevails over all other exigencies. Inversely, the contemplation of the images of death that are not subject to such imperatives is more private [*secret*], more *idiomatic*. Their observation is subject to individual and providential encounters (a visit to a museum, the chance discovery of an exhibition catalog). Their inscription in the collective memory is real (they belong to art history), but their inscription in the individual memory is more haphazard—and undoubtedly more infrequent. That is why these images do not *affect* us collectively in the same way. Their *sharing* is not identical. They do not participate in the formation of a selfsame *us*. This differentiation of affect and memorization is intensified by a differentiation in our relation to "the thought of death." These images do not make us *think of death* in the same way. One could say that they do not possess the same "contemplativity" [*pensivité*].

A third and final remark, then, concerns the political stakes of this *contemplativity* (or of its absence). As mentioned above, the images of death that "make the news" are the images of violent death (accidents, wars, epidemics, natural catastrophes, armed attacks, murders), similar to those found in much of the fiction (films and television series) that is foisted on us. Our everyday relation to death (assuming that these images still define a relation) is overdetermined by such images, which are more persistent, more frequent, and more simultaneous than any other experience of death. When we think of death, therefore, we do so, regardless of whether we want to, *with* a body affected by images that we have incorporated [*incorporés*], perhaps unknowingly, and which provoke by turn fascination, sadness, indignation, and anxiety. But such images, we should note, cannot be dissociated from the technical conditions of their production and diffusion. This means that, if we wish to focus thought on these images, we must reflect on the simultaneous proliferation of the affect that is orchestrated by their production and diffusion, and backed by sizable resources. This proliferation is constitutive of a collective memory that predetermines *our* relation to death—for example, *our* ability (or *our* inability), for any given death, to think of a name or to recall a face, singular, and irreducible to some kind of classification [*dénombrement*], calculation, or totalization.

These remarks leave us with a series of questions. What accounts for the contemplativity (or the non-contemplativity) of an image? What are the political effects and *expectations* of the various images? How, in each case, is the thought (or non-thought) of death shared (or not shared)? What "we" is being served? In order to sketch out elements of a response, I will concentrate again on the images evoked at the outset—that is, the images of death that, it is said, "make the news." Our long digression through *Phaedo* (however incomplete) will prove helpful in formulating the questions that these images evoke. Plato in effect teaches us at least two things. The first is that these images, however they affect us, are constitutive of a corporal memory that necessarily interferes with—if it does not obliterate or obfuscate— our "thought of death." The second is that all thought of death is simultaneously the thought of what life is *attached* to [*tient*], or of what we are *attached* to [*tenons*] in life. We should therefore ask of these images of death, of those that make the news (but the question is valid for the others as well), to what extent they are also referring us back to the thought of what makes life bearable [*tenable*] or unbearable [*intenable*], as life is exposed day after day to the *insufferable* [*insoutenable*].

To further the analysis of these images, three points must be emphasized. The first consists in recalling, with Jacques Derrida, that when we are exposed to these images of natural catastrophes, deadly attacks, war, epidemics, or spectacular accidents, we must realize that they constitute, in every instance, an *artifact*.[16] No doubt the "events" that they report are quite "real." There is no question of denying that they belong to the "world" in which we live. And yet two constitutive features should be highlighted. First, the fact that such images are selected primarily as "factual" [*événementiels*] is itself the result of a political and economic calculation and construction. "Events" are chosen, selected to make the news, because it is presupposed that they alone are susceptible of retaining our interest. They participate in the *capture* of our interest, the anticipation of which prescribes the definition and function of the media that relate them (television, magazines, etc.). The second feature, which calls for vigilance and to which we must be attentive, is that the "artifactuality" of the event is reinforced by that of the image. Not only the choice of the event, but also the selection and piecing together of images that are judged to cover the event, are constitutive of the news. In the absence of images capable of interesting *us*, the event could not be retained as such.

How then are we to understand why these images should evoke death so regularly and so massively, not that they necessarily show it (in the sense of focusing on the body—though they do just that on occasion),[17] but nevertheless do insist on referring to it? How is it that those who select these images, assemble them, and diffuse them presuppose, that is, calculate our interest in them? We recalled at the outset of our reflections that the frontier between the images of death that are diffused as news and those that, in perfect continuity, are imposed on us as entertainment, as fiction, is sometimes *undecidable*. This makes it difficult to differentiate between our supposed interest (assumed, anticipated, and programmed) in either the former or the latter. In the space of a single evening we pass from "real" death to "virtual" death—death by real catastrophes, accidents, and wars, to death by virtual catastrophes, accidents, and wars. The one is separated from the other by only a few advertisements.

We doubtless will say that we know how to distinguish between these various images—that we do not confuse the *unbearable* reality presented to us by the images that reveal "real" death and the virtual death that is exploited by fiction. And yet the two imageries are endlessly being translated into each other. Images of "real" dead that we are assumed to have consigned to memory and incorporated inspire the fictions that are offered to us. "Real" wars, "real" attacks, "real" catastrophes and accidents feed the creative imagination. We are invited to see in fictional images some aspect of present or past reality—or we are being asked to anticipate reality to come. Inversely, these "virtual dead" are not without an effect either on "reality" or on its presentation (that is to say, the montage of the news [*montage de l'actualité*]). Now and then someone will undertake to translate, *into reality*, the images that have taken possession of him through chance encounters with fictional presentations, as in video games.[18] One can sometimes trace the origin and explanation of killings, deadly attacks, and catastrophes to the virtual character of the images that inspired them. More generally we *find* in the news, as constructed—in the artifices of its construction according to some interest—some reflection of the fictions that are imagined, scripted, performed, filmed, mounted, programmed, marketed, and remarketed for our "entertainment."

The second point concerns the way we incorporate these images at the very site of their possible intermingling [*confusion*]—that is to say, in the way they affect our body. It would be false to think that such images are received and perceived indifferently, that their repetition as news or as fiction, year after year, leaves us unharmed. They fascinate [*fascinent*] us (even when they provoke pity or revulsion) and shape [*façonnent*] *us*. Nor do they work on us individually, but rather do so collectively. They are, proportionally to the technological means that are deployed to impose them, constitutive of this common memory of ours to which we are always compelled to return[19]— even if in the end we forget them as new "news" and new entertainments drive them away.

And yet these artifactual images do not aim at creating new affects. They do not seek to act on or influence our relation to the world directly—and even less our relation to death. They do not modify our memory in the slightest. On the contrary their fabrication conforms to a memory that is presupposed. Their fabrication presupposes affects that *we* are assumed to have already incorporated, in order not to shock *us,* disturb *us,* or trouble *us,* and thus keep *us tuned in* [*disponible*]. The images of death that are imposed on us, whether real or virtual, comply with the most general and common representation of death—to what we are *supposed* to be able to tolerate (i.e., have *already* tolerated). They are carefully dosed and formatted in accordance with a targeted memory.

The third point that we should bring up returns us to the thought of death. It concerns the singular relation of these images of death (images of war, assassinations, accidents, natural catastrophes) to death itself. Their logic, as we know, is one of quantification and bookkeeping. The images register the *number* of victims—the number, and not the singularity of the lives that have been brutally interrupted. It is the number that makes the "news." Of the dead evoked by the *news* day after day one must keep in mind, as discussed above, that we have no way to replace their number with names. We live with images of death whose primary effect is to deny the dead the capacity to evoke their singularity. One might well reply that it could not be otherwise, that the "news" does not have the means to enumerate [*énumérer*] all the dead of which it keeps a tally [*dénombre*]. And yet the images are there, and the *common memory* that they constitute, *with* which we live, is populated by nameless dead.

Because the dead, anonymous and indifferent, succeed one another in this memory—and because real death in this memory exists side by side with virtual death—this memory (artifactual and perhaps even artificial) is unsettling. Its images expose us (and perhaps habituate us) to the insufferable, while failing to provide us with the means to think about what, other than quantity, each death signifies singularly. And yet there is no thought of death that is not thought of its singularity. There is no thought that is not a confrontation with what in each death is *absolutely singular*. It is to this confrontation that Plato's *Phaedo* invites us, as does all great thought on death.[20] When we lose our sense of this irreducible singularity, when number replaces proper name, when it *makes the image* and when this image captivates us, fascinates us, and ultimately takes the place of thought, we lose all possibility of making the thought of death a thought of life—of what life *cares for* [*tient*], and of what we *care for* with life.

Exposure to *unbearable* images of death would be reasonable only if it led us to think about what is *borne* in each life singularly—and to think about what disappears with death: every time, for every life, *the world*. What is borne in each life, what each life bears in its own way, incomparable, irreducible to all belonging, is in effect nothing other than the world. Not one world among others (a world that another could replace), but, as we learn from our reading of Derrida, the world *in totality*.[21] Lacking such thought, it is appreciation of what is irreplaceable in each life that *we* lack—that is lacking in the *us* that *we* are. Lives, like the dead, become infinitely *substitutable, marketable,* and even *exploitable*. They become inscribed in the economies and calculations of war, terror, epidemics, and catastrophes, as well as in the economies and calculations surrounding the images of life and death that derive from such exploitation.

And yet such thought is not unfamiliar to us. We experience it every time when, on learning of the loss of someone close to us, we feel that the world has collapsed—and we *share* this "feeling" with others. In these moments of confusion, when our assurance stumbles, nothing is more unbearable than the idea that this disappearance of a loved one is simply the loss of one *world* among others. We cannot imagine, we do not want to imagine, that once the period of mourning has passed the world could *continue* as before—that it could remain the same. On the contrary, the disappearance of someone close always signifies for us that none of the cues and markers that were ours, in the time and the space of this world, can remain intact. But here a question arises that is eminently political, and is perhaps the question of politics itself. When do we cease to recognize in death (which deaths?) the collapse of the world? When do we cease to understand that this is the meaning of death for the one, or for those, who remain behind? When do we cease to understand that this significance does not apply merely to the disappearance of those who are close to me (family, friends), but to the disappearance of every human being?

We begin to grasp with greater clarity what is essentially at stake in the imagery of death (whether real or virtual). If it is true that such images are constitutive of a certain "memory of death"—notably of those violent deaths that are linked to war, terror, epidemics, catastrophes, and accidents—does their memorization, does the way that they necessarily affect our relation to death, enable us to think *the disappearance of each "victim," of each human being, without considera-tion of belonging, as the end of the world*? Or is it not, on the contrary, that their recurrence, their exploitation, their "commercialization," and the death-bearing [*mortifère*] culture that they organize contribute to the *eclipse* of such thought? In a sense, the journey that we have accomplished to this point has no other raison d'être than to bring us to this question. For prior to (and indeed summoning) the discus-sion of freedom and equality, it is the possibility and risk of such an *eclipse* that is at stake in politics. War, executions, whether *mass* exe-cutions or not, genocides, attacks (but also all forms of indifference, whether political, economic, or other, toward the victims of depriva-tions, poverty, epidemics), as well as all forms of encouragement, con-sent, and even resignation to the sacrifice of life, *assume this eclipse.* Just as do all calculations that make death acceptable, manageable, and ordinary, before it occurs as well as after. If calculations of this sort in effect entail the formation of a *we* (this enigmatic and perilous pronoun around which we have circled so often), if they can be de-ployed with substantial technical means, mobilized through expertise and copious imagery, the bond will, in the end, always and every-where be formed around such an *eclipse*—this is what unites.[22] This *we* is one of a "community" in (passive or active) agreement with the slaughter that its (political or religious) leaders organize. But it is also that of "entire peoples," indifferent or powerless spectators, who are resigned to these massacres, just as they put up with the death of a growing proportion of humanity by famine or disease, without access to food or medicine or the assistance that could save them. Thus death for *us,* for the *us* that finds itself constituted, inscribed in other considerations (economic, strategic, political, or religious), is no longer death. It no longer signifies, in its recurrences and proliferations, what it should always signify: the recurrent and proliferating disappearance, absurd and *unjust,* of the world, as borne singularly by each life. But by the same token it is also the world itself that such calculations forget or refuse (that *we* forget or refuse) to think about. What we have forgotten how to share is the meaning of the world. The eclipse of the meaning of death (and its sharing) and the eclipse of the meaning of the world (and its sharing) are indistinguishable.

Do such reflections reject [*récuse*] the imagery of death? Where this double eclipse would call for *another* memorization of death, and where, in doing so, it would invite us to remember *otherwise* what life holds dear [*ce à quoi tient la vie*] and what holds together with it [*ce qui tient avec elle*] and we know now that it is the world—the question of the imagery of death and its sharing reemerges with even greater consequence. It would in effect be wrong to deduce from these reflections that the image of death has been discredited and that a radical opposition has arisen between the "thought of death" and the "images of death." On the contrary, the critique of their use and the calculations (economic and political) behind that use has no consequence other than to suggest that we need *other* images, images thought *otherwise,* images that engage the thought of death *otherwise,* which supposes in reality another thought of, another *consideration* of the image itself.[23] In the presentations or representations of death (televisual, artifactual, or other), death in fact is not shown. It is eclipsed, to the benefit of other expectations that are not easily defined, but whose history has shown their implications for the kind of discrimination, violence, and injustice that have marked the last century (at a minimum).

In turn, this observation (which would have to be further developed, with illustrations from film and propaganda and news images) raises the following question. If the eclipse of the thought of death is all the more disastrous when it is buttressed by the exploitation of such images, how can, and how should death be shown so that there emerges from this very showing *another sharing* which would be simultaneously a *sharing of the meaning of the world and a sharing of the meaning of death*?

Notes

Introduction

[Translator's Acknowledgments: I wish to thank the Cultural Services of the French Embassy for their generous support of this project in the form of a French Voices grant, and Léa Surugue for indispensable editorial assistance.]

1. Sigmund Freud, *Reflections on War and Death,* trans. A. A. Brill and Alfred B. Kuttner (New York: Moffat, Yard, and Company), 1918.

2. Ibid., 11–12.

3. Ibid., 24.

4. Ibid., 34.

5. Ibid., 29–30.

6. Ibid., 47.

7. ["Primitive man" is used here and below to translate "l'homme originaire," following the English translation of Freud's essay. —*Trans.*]

8. Freud, *Reflections on War and Death,* 52.

9. Ibid., 58–60.

10. Ibid., 70. The numbering is my own. It seeks to underscore that, in a sense, the eight chapters that follow will have no other object than to deploy, in other ways, the meaning of these propositions and to draw conclusions from them.

11. Ibid.

12. ["The thought of death" will translate, throughout this book, the French *la pensée de la mort,* to connote a sustained, systematic, analytical contemplation or philosophy of death. —*Trans.*]

13. See chapter 2.

14. See chapter 4.

15. Derrida, as we will see in chapter 1, devoted a book, *Aporias* (Stanford: Stanford University Press, 1993), explicitly to the "deconstruction" of this passage. In this same vein, his readings of Blanchot and Celan, notably the latter's thought on "survivre" are indissociable from an implicit confrontation with Heidegger's thought on death. See chapter 5.

16. Françoise Dastur, *Death: An Essay on Finitude,* trans. John Llewelyn (London: Athlone, 2002); *How Are We to Confront Death?* trans. Robert Vallier (New York: Fordham University Press, 2012); *Comment vivre avec la mort?* (Paris: Pleins feux, 1998).

1. Being-toward-Death and Dasein's Solitude

1. [The term *partage* can mean sharing, dividing, or apportioning in French. All three terms will be used in this book in accordance with context. —*Trans.*]

2. Jacques Derrida, among others, undertook in *Aporias* to deconstruct this claim of superfluity.

3. See Martin Heidegger, *Being and Time,* trans. John Macquarrie and Edward Robinson (New York: Harper and Row, 1962), p. 308: "The non-relational character of death, as understood in anticipation, individualizes Dasein down to itself. This individualizing is a way in which the 'there' is disclosed for existence. It makes manifest that all Being-alongside the things with which we concern ourselves, and all Being-with Others, will fail us when our ownmost potentiality-for-being is the issue."

4. Ibid., 282.

5. Ibid., 284; *Sein und Zeit,* 240.

6. Heidegger, *Being and Time,* 294.

7. Ibid., 298.

8. Ibid.

9. Ibid.

10. I translate *Verfallen* by *chute* [fall] rather than by *dévalement* [tumble] (Vezin) or by *échéance* [sanction or forfeit] (Martineau), recalling that Heidegger takes care to specify that fall by his understanding has no relation at

all to that of Scripture (which should dispense the translator from having to innovate).

11. On the question of sacrifice, see chapters 2, 3, and 4.

12. See an analysis of this text in Marc Crépon, *Terreur et poésie* (Paris: Galilée, 2004).

13. Martin Heidegger, *The Hymns of Hölderlin: Germania,* trans. William McNeill and Julia Ireland (Bloomington: University of Indiana Press, forthcoming), n.p.

14. Ibid.; Martin Heidegger, *Hölderlins Hymnen "Germanien" und "Der Rhein"* (Frankfurt: Klostermann, 1980), 72.

15. Heidegger, *Hymns of Hölderlin,* n.p.; Heidegger, *Hölderlins Hymnen "Germanien" und "Der Rhein,"* 72–73.

16. Heidegger, *Being and Time,* 308–9.

17. On this point, see Crépon, *Terreur et poésie.*

18. See the text of Walter Benjamin, almost contemporary (1936) with the commentary on Hölderlin's hymns: "The Storyteller," in Walter Benjamin, *Illuminations,* trans. Harry Zohn, ed. Hannah Arendt (New York: Schocken, 1968), 84: "With the [First] World War a process began to become apparent which has not halted since then. Was it not noticeable at the end of the war that men returned from the battlefield grown silent—not richer, but poorer in communicable experience? What ten years later was poured out in the flood of war books was anything but experience that goes from mouth to mouth."

19. See Martin Heidegger, *Écrits politiques, 1933–1966,* trans. François Fédier (Paris: Gallimard, 1995), 114–15.

20. We should make it clear that in hazarding the expression "being against death," we do not intend to oppose the preposition "against" [*contre*] to the preposition "for" [*pour*] as it appears in the very problematic translation of *Sein-zum-Tode* as "être pour la mort" [Being-toward-death]. We know in effect that it would be inaccurate to assign a teleological signification to the preposition "pour" in this expression. In a letter to Hannah Arendt dated April 21, 1954, Heidegger asserted himself that this translation should be treated with caution.

21. I am writing this first chapter in 2001, at a time when, in Ukraine, a great part of the "people" bears witness to this "being-against-death" in an

extraordinary movement of resistance. It bears witness in several ways. There is a real sharing in the resistance forces and a mutual control of these forces so that they do not provoke a blood bath. Moreover, the movement itself is a struggle to assure that their vote is respected—a vote in which the desire for living conditions that would enable them to distinguish between, among other things, the common and equal protection on the one hand and the multiple forces of death on the other.

2. Dying-for

1. Jean-Paul Sartre, *Being and Nothingness,* trans. Hazel Barnes (New York: Washington Square Press, 1992), 682.

2. Ibid.

3. Ibid., 683: "The sleight of hand introduced by Heidegger is easy enough to detect." Sartre launches his critique of Heidegger's thought on Being-toward-death with these words. That critique will extend to about twenty pages.

4. Ibid., 682–83.

5. Ibid., 683.

6. Ibid., 684–85.

7. Jean-Paul Sartre, *The Flies,* Act II, in Sartre, *No Exit, and Three Other Plays* (New York: Vintage, 1949), 77.

8. Jean-Paul Sartre, *The Victors,* in Sartre, *Three Plays* (New York: Alfred A. Knopf, 1949), 213–14.

9. Jean-Paul Sartre, *Dirty Hands,* Act VII, in Sartre, *No Exit, and Three Other Plays,* 247.

10. See *The Victors,* Act I, p. 220: "CANORIS: Sorbier! I swear to you that you won't talk. You *couldn't* talk. / SORBIER: I tell you, I would have given up my own mother. [A pause] It's not fair that a single minute should be enough to ruin a whole life. / CANORIS [gently]: It takes much more than a minute. Do you think that a single moment of weakness could destroy that hour when you decided to leave everything and come with us? And these three years of courage and patience?"

11. Sartre, *Being and Nothingness,* 691.

12. Jean-Paul Sartre, *No Exit,* in *No Exit, and Three Other Plays,* 39.

13. Sartre, *Being and Nothingness,* 692.

14. Ibid.

15. Ibid., 695.

16. Ibid., 699.

17. Ibid., 693–94.

18. Ibid., 693.

19. Ibid., 692.

20. Jean-Paul Sartre, *The Words,* trans. Bernard Frechtman (New York: George Braziller, 1964), 255.

3. Vanquishing Death

1. Emmanuel Levinas, *Otherwise Than Being; or, Beyond Essence,* trans. Alphonso Lingis (Pittsburgh: Duquesne University Press, 1998).

2. See Emmanuel Levinas, "Dying for . . . " in Emmanuel Levinas, *Entre Nous: Thinking-of-the-Other,* trans. Michael B. Smith and Barbara Harshav (New York: Columbia University Press, 1998), 215: "But perhaps you also know that personal research and, notably, meditation on *Sein und Zeit,* have led me to thoughts which have never lost sight of that primordial book, though I have distanced myself from its thesis on the fundamental priority of ontology. I am not going to substitute these thoughts for the presentation of the Heideggerian ideas that are the main topic of this evening, but I will tell you, as I conclude, what matters to me. Very briefly. 'Dying for,' 'dying for the other.' I also considered calling my remarks 'dying together.'"

3. One should add to the texts mentioned here, among others, the lecture given at Louvain in 1982, *Éthique comme philosophie première* (Paris: Payot, 1992), with preface and notes by Jacques Rolland (not available in English).

4. Emmanuel Levinas, *Time and the Other,* trans. Richard A. Cohen (Pittsburgh: Duquesne University Press, 1987), 70.

5. Emmanuel Levinas, *God, Death, and Time,* trans. Bettina Bergo (Stanford: Stanford University Press, 2000), 36.

6. See ibid., 10: "And we must not decide too quickly that only nothingness is dreadful, as in a philosophy wherein man is a being who has to be, who persists in his being, without posing to himself the question of knowing what the dreadful and the dreaded are."

7. *Levinas, Time and the Other,* 71.

8. Ibid., 43.

9. *Leo Tolstoy, The Death of Ivan Ilyich,* in Tolstoy, *The Death of Ivan Ilyich, and Other Stories* (London: Penguin, 2008), 186.

10. Levinas, *Time and the Other,* 70 [translation slightly altered].

11. Ibid., 69 [translation slightly altered].

12. Tolstoy, *Death of Ivan Ilyich,* 215.

13. Of these three objections (see above), it is only the one that discusses anxiety as a fundamental affect, to the detriment of fear, which *Time and the Other* does not examine. It will be at the center of his analyses in *Totality and Infinity.* See below.

14. Levinas, *Time and the Other,* 72.

15. Ibid.

16. Emmanuel Levinas, *Totality and Infinity: An Essay on Exteriority,* trans. Alphonso Lingis (Pittsburgh: Duquesne University Press, 1969), 232.

17. Ibid., 233.

18. Ibid., 233–34.

19. Ibid., 234.

20. Ibid.

21. Ibid., 234–36.

22. Ibid., 236. Emphasis added by the author.

23. Honoré de Balzac's *La Peau de Chagrin* offers without doubt the most accurate and dramatic of parables of postponement, as conceived in these terms.

24. Levinas, *Totality and Infinity,* 236.

25. Levinas, *God, Death, and Time,* 13: "The problem we are posing here is the following: does the relationship to the death of the other not deliver its meaning, does it not articulate it by the depth of the affection, from the dread that is felt before the death of the other? Is it correct to measure this dreaded thing by the *conatus,* that is, by the persevering-in-my-being, by comparing it with the threat that weighs upon my being—that threat having been posited as the sole source of affectivity?"

26. Levinas, *Éthique comme philosophie première,* 96–97: Sean Hand and Michael Temple, trans., in Sean Hand, *The Levinas Reader* (Oxford: Blackwell, 1989), 83.

27. Levinas, *Éthique comme philosophie première,* 97–98: Hand and Temple,

trans., in Hand, *Levinas Reader,* 83–84: "Responsibility for the Other, for the naked face of the first individual to come along. A responsibility that goes beyond what I may or may not have done to the Other or whatever acts I may or may not have committed, as if I were devoted to the other man before being devoted to myself. Or more exactly, as if I had to answer for the other's death even before *being.*"

28. Levinas, "Dying for . . . ," 216. Emphasis added by the author.

29. Levinas, *Entre Nous,* 217. See, on this same point, "Notes on Meaning," in Emmanuel Levinas, *Of God Who Comes to Mind,* trans. Bettina Bergo (Stanford: Stanford University Press, 1998), which provides the last (or first) word on the mystery of death: "Responsibility for the other man, the impossibility of leaving him alone with the mystery of death, is concretely— across all the modalities *of giving*—the taking upon oneself [*susception*] of the ultimate gift of dying for another."

30. Levinas uses this expression, from *Time and the Other* forward, to discuss paternity, which I hope to examine in a future essay. See, on this theme, the analysis of Stéphane Moses, "Histoire et Paternité," in *Au-delà de la guerre: Trois études sur Levinas* (Paris: Éditions de l'Éclat, 2004).

4. Unrelenting War

1. See Franz Rosenzweig, "Globus: Studien zur weltgeschichtlichen Raumlehre," in *Zweistromland,* 313–48. See French translation in Marc Crépon et al., trans., *Confluences, politique, histoire, judaïsme* (Paris: Vrin, 2003). See also correspondence with Rosenstock in Marc Crépon et al., trans., *Foi et savoir, autour de l'Étoile de la redemption* (Paris: Vrin, 2001).

2. [The rather legalistic sounding "apportionment" will frequently be used to translate the French *partage.* The latter has connotations that the English "sharing" or "distribution" lack. It can connote "contest," the agonistic struggle of "get my share," as well as the altruistic sense of giving to the less fortunate, or the morally neutral "partake." It can also connote distribution as understood by the relevant English phrase "balance of power." "Power" in this chapter always translates *puissance.—Trans.*]

3. Jan Patočka, *Heretical Essays in the Philosophy of History,* trans. Erazim Kohák, ed. James Dodd (Chicago: Open Court, 1996), 121.

4. Ibid., 94. See also ibid., 123: "The revolution taking place here [in

Germany] had its deep driving force in the conspicuous scientification which all prewar experts on Europe and on Germany saw as the chief trait of its life: a scientification which understood science as technology, actually a positivism."

5. Jan Patočka, "The Dangers of Technicization in Science according to E. Husserl and the Essence of Technology as Danger according to M. Heidegger," trans. Erazim Kohák, in Kohák, *Jan Patočka: Philosophy and Selected Writings* (Chicago: University of Chicago Press, 1989), 336.

6. Patočka, *Heretical Essays,* 124–25.

7. Ibid., 129.

8. Ibid.

9. Ibid., 132.

10. See Marc Crépon, *Altérités de l'Europe* (Paris: Galilée, 2006).

11. See Marc Crépon, *La Culture de la peur: Identité, sécurité, démocratie* (Paris: Galilée, 2008).

12. Patočka, *Heretical Essays,* 133.

13. Patočka, "Dangers of Technicization in Science," 337. Emphasis added by the author.

14. Patočka, *Heretical Essays,* 130.

15. Ibid. Emphasis added by the author.

16. See ibid., 136: "[Heraclitus] did not mean thereby war as the expansion of 'life' but as the preponderance of the Night, of the will to the freedom of risk in the *aristeia,* holding one's own at the limit of human possibilities which the best choose when they opt for lasting fame in the memory of mortals in exchange for an ephemeral prolongation of a comfortable life."

17. Ibid., 134.

18. Ibid., 105. On this point, see Crépon, *Altérités de l'Europe,* chapter 6, "Le souci de l'Âme et l'héritage de l'Europe," 153–78.

19. See Patočka, *Heretical Essays,* 135: "The solidarity of the shaken is the solidarity of those who understand. Understanding, though, must in the present circumstances involve not only the basic level, that of slavery and of freedom with respect to life, but needs also to entail an understanding of the significance of science and technology, of that Force we are releasing. All the forces on whose basis alone can humans live in our time are potentially in the hands of those who so understand."

20. Ibid., 135.

5. The Imaginary of Death

1. Paul Ricœur, *Memory, History, Forgetting,* trans. Kathleen Blamey and David Pellauer (Chicago: University of Chicago Press, 2004), 357. To place this passage in the context of Ricœur's overall thought, see Frédéric Worms, "Vivant jusqu'à la mort . . . et non pas pour la mort," in *La pensée Ricœur,* special issue of the journal *Esprit,* April–May 2006, 304–16.

2. Paul Ricœur, *Living Up to Death,* trans. David Pellauer (Chicago: University of Chicago Press, 2009). In the postface of this posthumous work, Catherine Goldstein dates this text that we propose to examine in the following pages to early 1996. The "Fragments" that follow in the same volume date from the last months of Ricœur's life.

3. Ibid., 9.

4. It will fall to Jacques Derrida to "deconstruct" with great precision the presuppositions of Heidegger's authoritarian decision, according to which the interpretation of death, to the extent that it is ontological, must remain on "this side." See Derrida, *Aporias,* 54–57.

5. Ricœur, *Living Up to Death,* 15.

6. Ibid., 17.

7. Ibid., 14.

8. Ibid., 16.

9. [The play on words "living up to" as proposed by the English translation (with its suggestion of living "deservedly" of death) is not present in the French "*vivre jusqu'à la mort,*" "to live until death," hereafter translated in this chapter as "living unto death" (except, of course, as book title). —*Trans.*]

10. Norbert Elias, *The Loneliness of the Dying,* trans. Edmund Jephcott (New York: Continuum, 2001); and the book's postscript, "Ageing and Dying: Some Sociological Problems."

11. Ricœur, *Living Up to Death,* 17.

12. Ibid., 42.

13. Paul Ricœur, *Critique and Conviction, Conversations with François Azouvi and Marc de Launay,* trans. Kathleen Blamey (New York: Columbia University Press, 1998), 108. David Pellauer, in his translation of Ricœur, *Living Up to Death,* 25, offers this rendition of Semprún's phrase: "I seek the crucial region of the soul where absolute Evil and fraternity hang in the balance."

14. Ricœur, *Living Up to Death,* 23.

15. See ibid., 28: "*Every* death exterminates. This is what I take to be the third imaginary figure. It is not a simply fusion of death and the dying person, but catalyzes the *massa perdita* with absolute Evil."

16. See chapter 8.

17. Ricœur, *Living Up to Death,* 29–30.

18. Ibid., 38, 32.

19. Ibid., 40.

6. Fraternity and Absolute Evil

1. Jorge Semprún, *Literature or Life* (New York: Penguin Books, 1997), 14–15.

2. Ibid., 16–17. [The French suggests sharing, not apportionment. — *Trans.*]

3. See Ricœur, *Living Up to Death,* 26.

4. See Semprún, *Literature or Life,* 24: "Together we lived that experience of death, that compassion. This defined our being: to be with one another as death advanced upon us—or rather, ripened in us, spreading through us like a luminous poison, like an intense light that would obliterate us. All we who were going to die had chosen the fraternity of this death through a love of freedom."

5. Ibid., 18.

6. Ibid., 91.

7. On the evocation of the "Muslims" in the eyewitness accounts of the death camps, see Giorgio Agamben, *Remnants of Auschwitz: The Witness and the Archive,* trans. Daniel Heller-Roazen (New York: Zone Books, 2002), chapter 2.

8. Primo Levi, *If This Is a Man,* trans. Stuart Woolf (London: Abacus, 1987), 96. Emphasis added by the author.

9. See Zygmunt Bauman, *Wasted Lives: Modernity and Its Outcasts* (New York: Polity Press, 2004).

10. See Jacques Derrida, *The Politics of Friendship* (London: Verso, 2005). In chapter 9 of this work, titled "'In Human Language, Fraternity . . . ,'" Derrida discusses Jules Michelet's *The People* (Urbana: University of Illinois Press, 1973), and, on page 238, offers the following comments on the author's invocation of fraternity: "National singularity gives the example of universal

friendship or fraternity, the living example, the ideal example in the sense Cicero gives to the word *exemplar* in *De Amicitia*. And this is said universally in the French language, in which what is called, 'in human language, fraternity,' is uttered. To be exemplary, infinitely universal, French fraternity has as much need of being literal, singular, incarnate, living, idiomatic, *irreplaceable*, as fraternity *tout court* does, in order to become exemplary of universal fraternity, of being literally fraternal: that is to say, where a woman cannot replace a man, nor a sister a brother."

11. [Franz Rosenzweig, *Briefe*, ed. Edith Rosenzweig (Berlin: Schocken, 1935), 686: "Wo die Auserwähltheit Färbereagenz aller Nationalität überhaupt geworden ist, . . . ," which the author renders in French as "faire-valoir de toute nationalité," both here and in Franz Rosenzweig, *Foi et savoir, autour de l'Étoile de la rédemption* (Paris: Vrin, 2001), 91. A *Färbereagenz* is a "staining reagent" or tint. —*Trans.*]

12. Jacques Derrida, "Rams: Uninterrupted Dialogue—Between Two Infinities, the Poem," in *Sovereignties in Question: The Poetics of Paul Celan* (New York: Fordham University Press, 2005), 140.

13. Derrida, *Aporias*, chapter 1.

7. Hospitality and Mortality

1. Jacques Derrida, *Learning to Live Finally: The Last Interview*, trans. Pascale-Anne Brault and Michael Naas (Brooklyn: Melville House, 2007).

2. See Jacques Derrida, *The Work of Mourning*, ed. Pascale-Anne Brault and Michael Naas (Chicago: University of Chicago Press, 2001).

3. Jacques Derrida, *Memoires for Paul de Man*, rev. ed., trans. Cecile Lindsay, Jonathan Duller, Eduardo Cadava, and Peggy Kamuf (New York: Columbia University Press, 1986, 1989), 33–34.

4. See Jacques Derrida, "*Fors*: The Anglish Words of Nicolas Abraham and Maria Torok," foreword to Nicolas Abraham and Maria Torok, *The Wolf Man's Magic Word*, trans. Nicholas Rand (Minneapolis: University of Minnesota Press, 1986). On this point, see also Jacques Derrida, "Istrice 2: Ick bünn all hier," in *Points . . . Interviews, 1974–1994*, ed. Elisabeth Weber, trans. Peggy Kamuf et al. (Stanford: Stanford University Press, 1995), 321: "This is also what I call ex-appropriation, appropriation caught in a double bind: I must and I must not take the other into myself; mourning is an unfaithful

fidelity if it succeeds in interiorizing the other ideally in me, that is, in not respecting his or her infinite exteriority."

5. Derrida, *Memoires for Paul de Man,* 34.

6. Ibid., 33.

7. Jacques Derrida, *Adieu to Emmanuel Levinas,* trans. Pascale-Anne Brault and Michael Naas (Stanford: Stanford University Press, 1997), 23.

8. Derrida, quoting Levinas, in ibid., 27.

9. Derrida, *Memoires for Paul de Man,* 29.

10. Derrida, *Adieu to Emmanuel Levinas,* 32. Derrida quotes Emmanuel Levinas, "Peace and Proximity," trans. Peter Arterton and Sion Critchley, in *Emmanuel Levinas: Basic Philosophical Writings,* ed. Adriaan Peperzak et al. (Bloomington: Indiana University Press, 1996), 168.

11. Emmanuel Levinas, "The Nations and the Presence of Israel," in Levinas, *In the Time of the Nations,* trans. Michael B. Smith (Bloomington: Indiana University Press, 1994), 97: "Fraternity (but what does it mean? Is it not, according to the Bible, a synonym of humanity?) and hospitality: are these not stronger than the horror a man may feel for the other who denies him in his alterity? Do they not already bring back a memory of the 'Word of God'?"

12. Derrida devotes many pages to explaining how the thought of peace in the work of Levinas breaks with a whole tradition of thinking exemplified by the analyses of Kant. See *Adieu to Emmanuel Levinas,* 91: "Whereas for Kant the institution of peace could not but retain the trace of a warlike state of nature, in Levinas the inverse is the case, since allergy, the rejection of the other, even war, appear in a space marked by the epiphany of the face, where 'the subject is a host' and a 'hostage,' where unconsciousness of . . . , or intentional subjectivity, as responsible, traumatized, obsessed, and persecuted, first offers the hospitality that it is."

13. See Crépon, *La culture de la peur.*

14. Derrida, *Adieu to Emmanuel Levinas,* 85.

15. See ibid., 115: "It does not whisper silence over the necessity of a *relation* between ethics and politics, ethics and justice or law. *This relation is necessary,* it must exist, it is necessary to deduce a politics and a law from ethics. This deduction is necessary in order to determine the 'better' or the 'less bad,' with all the requisite quotation marks: democracy is 'better' than

tyranny. Even in its 'hypocritical nature,' 'political civilization' remains 'better' than barbarism." The necessity of such a deduction should give pause to those like Alain Badiou or Slavoj Žižek who, not content to reprove the present condition of democracies, reject the concept and call for a new tyranny. Such an appeal can occur only in the heedlessness of that which characterizes tyranny—in principle, that is, a politics of death that never, less often in any case than any other political regime, concerns itself with the mortality and vulnerability of "others," however one might define them (opponents, dissidents, etc.).

16. Ibid.

17. *The Work of Mourning,* a collection of Derrida's works edited by Michael Naas and Pascale-Anne Brault, published in English, came out in French under the title *Chaque Fois Unique, La Fin du Monde.*

18. *Unicité* in French, rarely employed, can mean unity or uniqueness, and thus suggests a play of words that the English cannot replicate.

19. Derrida, *Adieu to Emmanuel Levinas,* 98.

20. Ibid., 81.

21. On this point Derrida quotes a passage of Levinas's "The Nations and the Presence of Israel," 98: "To shelter the other in one's own land or home, to tolerate the presence of the landless and homeless on the 'ancestral soil,' so jealously, so meanly loved—is that the criterion of humanness? Unquestionably so." See Derrida, *Adieu to Emmanuel Levinas,* 73.

22. Derrida, *Aporias,* 39–40.

23. Ibid., 61.

24. See Derrida, *"Fors";* and Abraham and Torok, *Wolf Man's Magic Word.*

25. Derrida, "Istrice 2," 321.

26. Ibid.

27. See Derrida, *Aporias,* 76: "The death of the other thus becomes again 'first,' always first. It is like the experience of mourning that institutes my relation to myself and constitutes the egoity of the *ego* as well as every *Jemeinigkeit* in the *différance*—neither internal nor external—that structures this experience. The death of the other, this death of the other in 'me,' is fundamentally the only death that is named in the syntagm 'my death,' with all the consequences that one can draw from this. This is another dimension of awaiting [*s'attendre*] as awaiting one another [*s'attendre l'un l'autre*]."

28. In his last interview with *Le Monde,* Derrida uses the following terms to convey how *survivance* and originary mourning are linked in his thinking: "All the concepts that have helped me in my work, and notably that of the trace or of the spectral, were related to this 'surviving' as a structural and rigorously originary dimension. It is not derived from either living or dying. No more than what I call 'originary mourning,' that is, a mourning that does not wait for the so-called 'actual' death." See Derrida, *Learning to Live Finally,* 26.

29. Maurice Blanchot, *The Instant of My Death* / Jacques Derrida, *Demeure: Fiction and Testimony,* trans. Elizabeth Rottenberg (Stanford: Stanford University Press, 2000), 62–63.

30. Derrida, *Demeure,* 94.

31. Ibid., 95.

32. Ibid.

8. The Thought of Death and the Image of the Dead

1. [The French *actualité* is often translated "actuality." "Actuality" in English, however, is an uncommon, abstract-sounding term that contrasts with the frequently and widely employed *actualité,* which refers unproblematically to current events, as conveyed or constructed by *les informations,* the news. *Actualité(s)* is translated by "news" in this chapter except in cases where it gestures to a more general and abstract "actuality."—*Trans.*]

2. On this subject, see the excellent work by Susan Sontag, *Regarding the Pain of Others* (New York: Picador, 2004), in which the author asks from the outset (and answers immediately), in terms that are somewhat different from those proposed here, "Who are the 'we' at whom such shock-pictures are aimed? That 'we' would include not just the sympathizers of a smallish nation or a stateless people fighting for its life, but—a far larger constituency—those only nominally concerned about some nasty war taking place in another country" (7).

3. Jacques Derrida reminds us in an interview given to the review *Passages* (vol. 57, September 1993), reprised in the beginning of Jacques Derrida and Bernard Stiegler, *Echographies of Television,* trans. Jennifer Bajorek (Cambridge: Polity, 2002), 4: "Among the filterings that 'inform' actuality and despite an accelerated but all the more equivocal internationalization, there is this ineradicable privilege of the national, the regional, the provincial—

or the Western—which overdetermines all the other hierarchies (first sports, then the 'politician'—and not the political—then the 'cultural,' in supposedly decreasing order of demand, spectacularity, and legibility). This privilege relegates to a secondary position a whole host of events: those thought to be too far removed from the nation's (supposedly public) interest, from its vicinity, from the national language, code, and style."

4. This paragraph obviously refers once again to Heidegger's analyses of Being-toward-death in paragraphs 46–53 of *Being and Time*. See the reading proposed by Dastur, *Death*; and Derrida, *Aporias*.

5. Jacques-Bénigne Bossuet, "Sermon on Death," http://www.thomas morecollege.edu/wp-content/uploads/2009/07/Bossuet-Sermon-on-Death.pdf, page 1: "It may even be said that mortals take no less care to bury the thoughts of death than they do the dead themselves." On Nietzsche, see the astonishing section 278 of *The Gay Science,* trans. Walter Kaufmann (New York: Vintage, 1974), 224–25: "Everyone wants to be the first in this future—and yet death and deathly silence alone are certain and common to all in this future. How strange it is that this sole certainty and common element makes almost no impression on people, and nothing is further from their minds than the feeling that they form a brotherhood of death."

6. On contemporary modalities of this absence of sharing, see Norbert Elias's sociological analysis in *The Loneliness of Dying,* trans. Edmund Jephcott (New York: Continuum, 1985).

7. Plato, *Phaedo*, 63 C, D, trans. Harold North Fowler (Cambridge: Harvard University Press, 2005), 219. Emphasis added by the author. ["Share" in the French edition is rendered as *partageras.—Trans.*]

8. Ibid., 67 D, 235. Emphasis added by the author. Translation slightly modified by the translator in conformity with both the author's and Plato's text.

9. Ibid., 68 C, 237.

10. On death as the interruption of dialogue, see Derrida, "Rams: Uninterrupted Dialogue."

11. Plato, *Phaedo,* 81 A, 283.

12. Ibid., 81 B, 283.

13. Ibid., 80 E, 281.

14. On Callot's and Goya's works, see Sontag, *Regarding the Pain of Others,* chapter 3.

15. I have in mind two oil paintings on wood by Antonio de Pereda: *The Knight's Dream* (Madrid, Real Academia de San Fernando) and *The Allegory of Transience* (Vienna, Kunsthistorisches Museum). The first represents a young nobleman, richly attired, asleep, his head resting on the palm of his hand. On a table cast in shadow are displayed the objects of his dream (a globe, a crown, armor, coins, a mask, a weapon, flowers)—all things desirable—and, in their midst, a human skull. Beside the knight an angel deploys a banner on which is written: *Aeterne pungit, cito volat et occidit* (Eternally stings, swiftly flies and kills). Such an image of death is inseparable from its contemplativity [*pensivité*]. It displays its function, which is to push us to *think* about death, giving rise to a whole series of questions, which, in fact, are the same as those questions that are posed by every image of death: How is this thoughtfulness organized? Who commands it? To whom is it addressed?

16. See Derrida and Stiegler, *Echographies of Television*, 3: "Actuality is, precisely, *made* [*faite*]: in order to know what it's made of, one needs nonetheless to know that it is made. It is not given but actively produced, sifted, invested, performatively interpreted by numerous apparatuses which are *factitious* or *artificial,* hierarchizing and selective, always in the service of forces and interests to which 'subjects' and agents (producers and consumers of acutality—sometimes they are 'philosophers' and always interpreters, too) are never sensitive enough. No matter how singular, irreducible, stubborn, distressing or tragic the 'reality' to which it refers, 'actuality' comes to us by way of a fictional fashioning."

17. The question, what constitutes a "show" of death and, even more, of the dead, would require a study in and of itself. When, how, and on what condition does one show "cadavers"? And when one does so, how does one show them? From the back, from the front, the face covered? See again, on this point, the very enlightening analyses of Sontag in *Regarding the Pain of Others,* chapter 4.

18. The most significant example is the Columbine massacre in the United States, a striking image of which is provided by the Gus Van Sant film *Elephant* (inspired by real facts that were informed by virtual, electronic-game deaths).

19. On the constitution of this shared memory, and on the technical techniques that give rise to it, its political and economic stakes, see the works of

Bernard Stiegler, notably *De la misère symbolique I: L'époque hyperindustrielle* (Paris: Galilée, 2004).

20. I'm thinking notably of the relevant paragraphs (46–53) of Heidegger's *Being and Time,* and to the commentaries on those paragraphs in Derrida's *Aporias* or Dastur's *Death.*

21. See chapters 6 and 7. On this point, see Derrida, "Rams: Uninterrupted Dialogue"; as well as *Chaque fois unique, la fin du monde* (Paris: Galilée, 2003), 9: "The death of the other, not only but especially if one loves him, does not announce an absence, a disappearance, the end *of such or other* life, that is, of the possibility for a world (always unique) to appear to *some* living person. Death declares each time the death of the world in totality, the end of any possible world, and *each time the end of the world as unique totality, thus irreplaceable and thus infinite.*" [From Derrida's avant-propos to the French edition of Derrida, *The Work of Mourning.*]

22. The analysis of the mechanisms that led to the genocide of the Tutsis and the Hutu opposition in Rwanda (and this could also be said of the wars in the Balkans) provides a frightening attestation to this *eclipse.* On this topic, see the eyewitness accounts provided by executioners in Jean Hatzfeld, *Machete Season* (New York: Picador, 2006).

23. On this point, see Jean-Luc Nancy, *The Ground of the Image,* trans. Jeff Fort (New York: Fordham University Press, 2005). If we had to go further in this direction, some of the orientations provided by this book would well be worth exploring. We should recall that it concludes with a meditation on the images of death, specifically.

Index

Marc Crépon is director of the philosophy department at École Normale Supérieure and director of research at the Archives Husserl. He is the author of sixteen books.

Michael Loriaux is professor of political science at Northwestern University. He is the author, coauthor, and coeditor of several books, including *Law and Moral Action in World Politics* (Minnesota, 2000).

Rodolphe Gasché is Eugenio Donato Chair of Comparative Literature at the University at Buffalo, State University of New York. He is the author of several books, including *The Tain of the Mirror: Derrida and the Philosophy of Reflection* and *Georges Bataille: Phenomenology and Phantasmatology*.